FRESH & HEALTHY
COOKING FOR TWO
EASY MEALS FOR EVERYDAY LIFE

ELLIE TOPP,
MSc, PHEc, CCP

&

MARILYN BOOTH,
MSc, RD

FORMAC PUBLISHING COMPANY LIMITED
HALIFAX

Watch our video clips to go behind-the-scenes with Chef Michael Howell!

 Look for this symbol next to your favourite recipes or check www.formac.ca/videos for a complete list.

Formac Publishing Company Limited recognizes the support of the Province of Nova Scotia through the Department of Tourism, Culture and Heritage. We acknowledge the financial support of the Government of Canada through the Canada Book Fund for our publishing activities.

NOVA SCOTIA
NOUVELLE-ÉCOSSE
Tourism, Culture and Heritage
Tourisme, Culture et Patrimoine

The Canada Council | Le Conseil des Arts
for the Arts | du Canada

Library and Archives Canada Cataloguing in Publication

Topp, Ellie, 1938-
    Fresh & healthy cooking for two : easy meals for everyday life /
Ellie Topp and Marilyn Booth.

Issued also in electronic format.
ISBN 978-0-88780-982-8

    1. Cooking for two. 2. Quick and easy cooking.
3. Cookbooks. I. Booth, Marilyn II. Title.
III. Title: Fresh and healthy cooking for two.

TX833.5.T657 2011   641.5'612   C2011-904208-8

Formac Publishing Company Limited
5502 Atlantic Street
Halifax, Nova Scotia
B3H 1G4
www.formac.ca

Printed and bound in China.

Photo Credits

T=top, B=bottom, C=centre, L=left, R=right

Photography by Jen Partridge, Partridge Photography with the following exceptions:

Elżbieta Sękowska: 27; Ina Peters: 16TL, 29, 50TL, 65, 85, 140TC, 151; iStockphoto: 3, 4, 6, 7, 8, 9, 10, 11, 12, 13, 14, 15, 16TR, 23, 58, 63, 73, 77, 139; Jacob Van Houten: 21, 97; Jean Gill: 20, 67, 75; Lucía Cóppola: 30; Sasha Fox Walters: 33

CONTENTS

Mealtime is a time for relaxation,

to pause and reflect on the day's activities while sharing good conversation and good food. Not only do good foods make for pleasurable moments, they also hold the promise of good health. If you are two, making a meal with enough, but not too much, is an enjoyable process with a gratifying result. Cooking for two can be as imaginative as preparing for a dinner party, while retaining the simplicity we want when preparing everyday meals. That's the approach we've taken in this book.

Here you'll find a variety of delicious recipes designed for two. These dishes are easy to prepare and make use of fresh ingredients found in most kitchens. Dinner for two has never been easier!

These meals are designed to be enjoyable — and to be healthy too. We've made the nutritional information simple to refer to.

You'll find new takes on a wide variety of old favourites, as well as some less familiar ingredients, such as quinoa and edamame. Each dinner recipe features suggestions for simple, tasty side dishes. Feel free to mix and match these suggestions for an adventurous exploration of the world of food and flavour.

We hope you enjoy our simple, tasty, small-scale solutions to easy meals for everyday life!

Eating Great-Tasting Healthy Food

The recipe selection in this book offers new, simple ways to create quick, healthy meals which follow Canada's Food Guide. It has never been so easy to get the vitamins, minerals and nutrients you need to achieve good health and vitality. The recipes help you eat well by following the time-proven rule of variety, balance and moderation. For more details on Canada's Food Guide check out their website.

Vegetables and Fruit

Brighten up your meal — the more colours of vegetables and fruit you eat, the better! Take a look in your basket or cart at the grocery store — if it's full of colourful produce you're doing well; if one colour dominates, consider swapping out a few items. That bright orange of carrots and squash and the vivid red of tomatoes come from beta carotene and lycopene, respectively, two important phytochemicals. Other vegetable super-powers are members of the cabbage family including broccoli, cauliflower and rapini with plentiful amounts of Indoles and sulforaphane. These compounds found in plants are also phytochemicals that are associated with good health in humans. Some phytochemicals act as antioxidants, combining with free radicals in our bodies and limiting any harm they might cause.

Not only are vegetables and fruit cancer fighters, their abundance

of vitamins and minerals boosts immunity. As well, their folate helps form body cells and the minerals they contain such as potassium and calcium help to control blood pressure and build stronger bones.

Every vegetable and fruit has its own mix of health promoters. So getting a variety ensures that you take advantage of the goodness they have to offer. Surprisingly, when choosing vegetables and fruit, fresh is not always best. Certainly during the growing season, nothing beats vegetables fresh from the garden or fruit from the tree. But during the winter months, frozen vegetables and fruit can be a better choice. These are processed only a short time after picking, thereby "locking in" their nutrients. Nutrients in fresh produce begin to decline immediately after picking so foods that travel long distances may not offer all the benefits of their frozen relatives — not to mention the carbon footprint of all that travel.

Health organizations advocate a diet high in vegetables, fruit and other plant-based foods. Canada's Food Guide suggests 7 to 10 servings daily, so for continuing good health, resolve to plan your meals around colourful vegetables and fruit.

The Seven Challenge

Here are some easy, tasty ways to reap the benefits of the vegetable and fruit food group, with at least seven servings a day.

- Start the day with a banana or berries on cereal.
- Make a batch of soup for lunch or a light supper such as Quick Vegetable Egg-Drop Soup for One (page 120) or Sherried Cream of Broccoli and Other Vegetable Soups (page 128). On warm days, enjoy a bowl of cool, refreshing Gazpacho (page 124).
- Serve simple-to-prepare salads with your dinners. Check out Spinach Salad with Orange Ginger Dressing (page 75) and Quick Savoy Coleslaw (page 60).
- Add interest with a variety of vegetables. Try Peas and Kohlrabi Combo (page 98), Sliced Brussels Sprouts with Parmesan (page 85) and Baked Squash Rings with Ginger-Honey Glaze (page 83).
- Enjoy fruit for dessert and keep a basket of fruit for between meal nibbling.
- For snacking, make a trail mix with nuts, whole grain cereal and plenty of dried fruit like apricots, raisins and chopped cranberries.

Choose a different vegetable and fruit each day. Focus on those that are brightly coloured like broccoli, kale, red peppers, sweet potatoes, oranges, tomatoes, strawberries and blueberries. You will enjoy not only the health benefits, but also the great, fresh taste.

Grains

Grains and the myriad of foods made from them are an excellent source of energy. Some of the great cuisines of the world are founded on grains, from bread to tortillas, and from pasta to rice. Think Thai noodles, Indian chapattis and Scottish oatcakes to name only a few. Considered for many years to be only a companion, never the star of the meal, more recently grains have come into their own.

Carbohydrates

Grains offer a wide range of vitamins and minerals as well as protein, but the main contribution of grains is carbohydrate. Carbohydrates are our major source of energy. It is recommended that 40 to 60 per cent of your energy come from carbohydrate-rich foods.

Carbohydrates are found in a wide variety of foods and were formerly divided into two categories: complex carbs such as whole grains and pasta, which were once considered the best choice, and simple carbs like sugar and honey, considered not so great. A newer system, the glycemic index, classifies carbohydrates based on how quickly they boost blood sugar levels compared to pure glucose, a simple sugar. Foods that cause rapid spikes in blood sugar, like bread, have a high glycemic index. Low glycemic index foods, such as whole grains and legumes, bring on a slower rise in blood sugar. A related concept, the glycemic load, calculates the actual amount of carbohydrate in a food and its impact on blood sugar. Neither the complex-simple classification of carbohydrates nor the glycemic system provides a hard and fast guide to dietary choices. A better guide is to choose whole foods that include the fibre-rich outer layer as well as the nutrient-filled germ of the kernel.

Fibre

Along with vegetables, fruit and legumes, the grain family offers the ever-important fibre. Fibre has two forms — insoluble in water and soluble. Insoluble fibre is the form most effective in regulating our gastrointestinal function. The bran layers from all grains are the most familiar example along with the skins of vegetables and fruit. A diet with lots of insoluble fibre helps prevent constipation, haemorrhoids and diverticular disease by adding bulk and helping speed the transit of food through the gut.

Soluble fibre inside the intestine combines with cholesterol and eliminates it, helping lower blood cholesterol levels. By slowing the absorption of food from the digestive tract, soluble fibre also slows the release of glucose into the body, keeping blood sugar at stable levels. Vegetables and fruit contain this important nutrient, especially high-pectin fruit such as apples. Legumes and whole grains, notably oats and barley, contain soluble fibre as well as the insoluble type.

In addition to health benefits, both soluble and insoluble fibre help satisfy the appetite by providing a feeling of fullness. The daily reference value for fibre ranges from 21 to 38 grams based on the calories in your diet. In order to reach that goal, look for foods labelled "high" or "very high" in fibre. A very high source of fibre must contain at least 6 grams of fibre per serving and a high source at least 4 grams. Apple Cinnamon Raisin Bran Muffins (page 29) have 4 g of fibre per muffin while Cranberry Pancakes with Oat Bran and Flax (page 28) deliver 9 g per serving.

Whole Grains

To make the best whole grain choice, check the ingredient list on all packaged foods. Ingredients are always listed in descending order with the most prevalent ingredient listed first. Many so-called "multi-grain" breads feature enriched wheat flour as the first ingredient rather than a whole grain flour. Look for the term "whole grain wheat" to be high on the list.

As civilizations developed, grains were often refined by removing much of the bran layer, which discarded many of the beneficial vitamins and minerals along with the fibre. Indeed, the modern processing of wheat is one of the dubious technological advances of the Industrial Revolution. To compensate for the loss of nutrients during milling and grinding, government regulations require that thiamin, riboflavin, niacin and folate as well as iron are added back into refined enriched grain products such as white flour, pasta and cornmeal. Of course, there are times when only a white crusty baguette or hot biscuits will do. But except for these special occasions, it is worth discovering the savoury world of whole grains.

Folate

Folate, one of the B vitamins, is involved in the production of DNA and plays a major role in the formation of cells. Because red blood cells are replaced frequently, a shortage of folate is often detected as a form of anemia. As well, folate made nutritional news when it was shown to reduce the risk of certain defects in the rapidly growing fetus.

The suggested intake of folate is 400 mcg per day. Enriched grain products are important, but equally important is getting folate from the other foods. Eating fruit, leafy green vegetables and legumes every day should provide enough folate to meet the requirements of most people. To be sure, serve legumes at least once a week along with lots of leafy veggies. Hummus in Pita Pockets (page 40), Soup with Lentils, Fresh Herbs and Kale (page 130) and Thai-Style Edamame and Veggies (page 112) offer tasty ways to fulfill this goal.

Ancient and Modern Grains

Recently, many non-traditional, ancient grains have become available, including quinoa, spelt and kammut. And many familiar grains can now be found in interesting forms, such as wheat and rye berries, cracked wheat and bulgur. These grains are perfect for adding interest and variety to your meals. Try Tabbouleh with Feta and Grape Tomatoes (page 36), or Quinoa Pilaf with Fennel (page 70) for a delicious way to include healthy carbohydrates in your diet.

Milk

Since prehistoric times when farmers first began herding animals, milk has been an integral part of most traditional diets. Consumed alone or in recipes, milk products provide unique taste, texture and variety. Along with culinary benefits, milk offers an array of important nutrients — carbohydrate, protein, vitamins and minerals, especially calcium. From a cold beverage to marvellous cheeses and yogurts, there are many ways to enjoy milk.

Yogurt has become a very popular dairy product. Most yogurts contain live bacteria and some have special types added in order to give possible health benefits. Whether all of the claims made for these "probiotic" foods are valid is an open question. But whatever the health benefits, yogurt is a great asset in the kitchen. Cabbage Apple Salad with Yogurt Dressing (page 62), Raspberry Yogurt Parfait (page 146) and Mango Fool with Blueberries (page 150) are tasty examples.

While savouring milk in its many forms, keep in mind that the fat is primarily the saturated kind. So choose lower fat products and enjoy the higher fat forms sparingly. Fat-reduced evaporated milk, with twice the nutrients of regular milk, is marvelous for adding creaminess to soups and sauces. Check out Fish Chowder with Vegetables (page 136).

Calcium

Milk is the leading food source of calcium, essential for people of all ages. Stored mostly in our bones and giving them strength, calcium is the most abundant mineral in the body. Small children require calcium for their growing bodies. People over the age of 50, especially women, also have increased requirements, and are recommended to take in 1,200 mg per day. As people age, bone density decreases, making the threat of osteoporosis a real one. Calcium also helps protect against high blood pressure, heart disease and colon cancer.

Without milk products, meeting our calcium needs is a major challenge. Not all calcium sources are equal — calcium from dairy products is readily available, unlike that from plant-based foods. While vegetables, nuts and legumes do offer calcium, it takes about 5 cups (1.25 L) of cooked green beans, broccoli or Brussels sprouts to equal the calcium in one glass of milk!

Enjoyable ways to get the calcium you need:
- Try a delicious Fresh Fruit and Fibre Breakfast Smoothie (page XX) to start your day.
- Add evaporated milk to recipes calling for regular milk for twice the calcium.
- Top steamed vegetables, soups and casseroles with grated cheese.
- Top fruit desserts with plain or vanilla yogurt.
- End the day with a warm mug of milk flavoured with chocolate or Ovaltine.

Vitamin D

In addition to calcium, milk is fortified with vitamin D, making milk our main food source of this important nutrient. Vitamin D is a necessary companion to calcium for bone health and ongoing research suggests that vitamin D may offer protection against other illnesses. Sunshine on our skin allows our bodies to make vitamin D, but for many of us, especially those living in northern climates, supplements may be needed to augment that in fortified milk and soy beverages. As it unfolds, this will be a story to follow.

Meat, poultry, fish, eggs, beans, nuts & more

Meat, fish, eggs and legumes are protein powerhouses. But while this food group provides many other important nutrients, a little goes a long way, so use it sparingly. We need just 150 grams or 5 ounces of cooked meat or equivalent alternative daily according to Canada's Food Guide. The choices are many for this group: the familiar beef, pork, chicken, turkey and fish, but also the many types of beans, lentils, nuts and seeds. Variety is the key. It is good to choose meat alternatives frequently, but keep in mind that without the occasional appearance of meat on your plate, it is easy to experience a shortage of vitamin B_{12}, iron and zinc. Almost all our vitamin B_{12} comes from animal sources and iron and zinc are more readily available in meat than from plant sources. So choose quality over quantity and think of planning your meal around vegetables and whole grains with meat or alternatives adding flavour and interest. There's no need to give up a celebration steak dinner — just watch the portion size.

The call for moderation in meat consumption stems from the saturated fat in many animal products. Select lean cuts of beef and trim all the fat you can from pork and lamb. Removing the skin either before or after cooking decreases the fat from roast chicken and poultry. While the white meat of poultry is generally lean, keep in mind that the fat content of ground chicken or turkey can be surprisingly high if it is made from untrimmed higher-fat dark meat.

While buying lean is important, cooking lean is even more so. A cast iron or nonstick skillet is a must for low-fat cooking. Broiling and microwaving are also good choices to minimize the fat of this food group. And use sauces that add flavour while limiting added fat and calories. Southwest Taco Beef over Rice (page 78) and Chicken with Wine and Sweet Potatoes (page 72) are good examples.

Fish

Since the mid-1900s seafood has become increasingly popular, partly because fish and shellfish are no longer limited to a few familiar species. Today grocery stores and fish markets display a phenomenal array of choices.

Fish is popular because it is delicious, and it has nutritional value along with its relatively low calorie and fat content. Lean fish such as sole and haddock bring hardly any fat except that introduced in cooking. But it is the fatty fish such as salmon and sardines that are making the most nutritional news. Fat from fish contains two special omega-3 fatty acids — eicosapentaenoic acid (EPA) and docosahexaenoic acid (DHA) — that offer definite health benefits. These fats have been shown to slow the progression of heart disease. They may also help keep blood pressure in check and modify the inflammatory responses that cause conditions like arthritis and asthma.

So wise advice is to eat fish once or twice a week. Easy to prepare, fish is a perfect choice for two. Our favourites are Salmon with Dijon and Sesame Glaze (page 94), Quick Fish and Vegetables En Papillote (page 100) and Fish Chowder with Vegetables (page 136).

Eggs

Eggs deserve a significant place on our menus. While the high quality of egg protein is well known, the other nutrients eggs provide are often overlooked. With the exception of vitamin C, egg yolks contribute to the full range of the vitamins and minerals we need for good health, along with lutein and zeaxanthin, two carotenoids associated with eye health.

Egg yolks were given a bad name before the role of dietary cholesterol on blood cholesterol was well understood. It is now accepted that the main dietary cause of increased blood cholesterol is the amount of saturated fat in food. The fat in eggs is a blend of the desirable monounsaturated kind with less than one-third being saturated. More recently omega-3 eggs have become popular. While not nearly as rich in DHA as fish, every little bit counts.

Eggs offer an added benefit for the cook as they are quick and easy to prepare. Dress them up as Healthier Eggs Benedict (page 18) for a special weekend breakfast. Or think omelettes and frittatas enhanced by vegetables and a bit of cheese as in Mini-Frittata with Ham, Sweet Red Pepper and Plum Tomato (page 47).

Soy and Beans

Another highly valued alternative to meat is the legume family. Legumes are diverse, user friendly and happily absorb the flavours of other foods. In addition to providing sufficient protein to be considered meat alternatives, they are also packed with vitamins, minerals, phytochemicals and fibre, usually accompanied by very little fat. Folate and iron are two of their significant contributions. As a source of fibre, they rate next to bran cereals, with a good mix of both the insoluble and soluble kind. Since they are digested slowly, legumes bring about a slow rise in blood sugar, a benefit for those with diabetes.

Soybeans are unique among the legumes in that the protein in soy is high quality. Soy protein has also been found to have a protective effect on the heart, and as part of a low-fat diet, soybeans may help to lower blood cholesterol. Soybeans also contain more calcium than most other legumes but also more oil and of course, more calories.

One benefit of soy, animal and fish proteins comes from the fact that they are complete proteins containing all the amino acids our bodies need. The human body can make many of the amino acids it needs for growth and repair, but there are nine, called essential amino acids, that must come from our food. With the exception of soybeans, the protein in legumes, while abundant, has one or more of the essential amino acids in short supply.

This problem of limited essential amino acids is easily solved. Grains are also low in some of the essential amino acids, and, as luck would have it, the amino acids lacking in legumes are generously supplied by those in grains, and vice versa. This mutually advantageous relationship between grains and legumes gives rise to the concept of complementary proteins, whereby the amino acid pattern of one is balanced by the amino acid pattern of the other. Keep this relationship in mind and serve a meal featuring beans (legumes) with a slice of fresh artisan bread (grain). Other combinations are the Barley Lentil Bake with Mushrooms (page 114) and Brazilian Beans and Rice (page 54) where barley or rice, both grains and legumes in the form of beans and lentils simmer together for a tasty meal.

Portion Size

Select from the meat and alternatives group without allowing them to overwhelm your plate. One serving should be approximately the size of a deck of cards. For most of us, two servings a day for a total of 5 ounces or 150 grams should do the trick. And bring in fish, eggs, legumes and nuts to share the limelight. In general, 2 1/2 ounces (75 grams) of cooked fish, shellfish, poultry or lean meat, 3/4 cup (175 mL) cooked legumes, 2 eggs, 2 tablespoons (30 mL) peanut butter or 1/4 cup (60 ml.) shelled nuts or seeds can be considered equivalents.

Fat

Contrary to popular press, fat is not a nutrient to be avoided. Vital to our cells and hormones, and for the absorption of certain vitamins, fat is essential to good health. In food, fat is associated with taste and texture, giving creaminess to soups and sauces and tenderness to baking and meats. Think of the olive and its oil that are largely responsible for the exceptional flavours of Mediterranean cuisine. It is the type of fat we eat that is important to health, although moderation remains the key message.

Canada's Food Guide recommends two to three tablespoons (30 to 45 mL) of unsaturated fat daily. So first, a bit of chemistry. The fat in food is made up of fatty acids that are either saturated, monounsaturated or polyunsaturated. Saturated fats are associated with elevated blood cholesterol levels. In general, foods high in saturated fats are solid at room temperature, such as butter and lard. Research has shown that monounsaturated and polyunsaturated fats have a beneficial role in regulating blood cholesterol, especially the LDL ("bad") cholesterol. Olive, canola and safflower are oils with substantial amounts of monounsaturated fat. For salad dressings and cooking, these are the oils to choose. Thus, for your salad bowl, a good vinaigrette is a healthier choice than many dressings that are labelled low-fat.

Trans fats are formed when hydrogen is added to vegetable oils to make the oil solid at room temperature as in the manufacture of margarine. Recent research has linked artificially produced trans fats to health concerns, especially increased levels of LDL cholesterol and lower levels of HDL ("good") cholesterol. Check food labels for trans fats and for any ingredient called "hydrogenated." In *Fresh & Healthy Cooking for Two*, canola and olive oils are used in most of our recipes, with butter used sparingly for flavour.

Not all trans fats result from food manufacturing. Conjugated linoleic acid (CLA) is a naturally occurring trans fat, formed in ruminant animals such as cows and present in their meat and milk products. In studies with animals, CLA has shown promise in lowering the risk of chronic disease. CLA may also promote leanness and ward off diabetes. As research progresses, this may be an interesting story.

Salt

Salt has been a preservative and flavour enhancer since humans first discovered that crystals from seawater made foods taste much better. While humans need a little salt, the question remains "how much is not so good?" Table salt is made of sodium chloride with the sodium part being the concern, whether from salt, baking soda, monosodium glutamate or other additives.

Sodium has been linked to high blood pressure, but is not the only cause. Maintaining a healthy weight, being moderately active and eating well can be protective. But some individuals are especially salt sensitive, responding adversely to even a relatively low-sodium diet.

Scientists reviewing the best research have not been able to establish a clear-cut nutrient requirement for sodium. As a result, an Adequate Intake (AI) was established for sodium rather than a Recommended Dietary Allowance (RDA). The current AI for sodium is 1,500 mg per day (about two-thirds of a teaspoon) for those up to age 50, and less for those older and for young children.

In Canada, the Consumer Packaging and Labelling Act regulates the information on food labels. For sodium, the per cent daily value is based on 2,400 mg rather than 1,500 mg per day. To be consistent with food labels, we used the same base in our nutrition tables. Take note that the per cent daily value understates the sodium content for all foods. Keep your eye on the amount of salt in milligrams, and aim for the target of 1,500 mg per day — and less if you're over 50.

The bottom line for salt is moderation unless you have a medical condition dictating severe restriction. But the salt shaker is probably the least of your worries; the hidden salt in fast and prepared foods is the real concern. Most commercial foods and restaurant meals are well salted — in elegant restaurants as well as fast-food outlets. If canned soups and other packaged foods are frequent items on your menu, your sodium intake may hit more than 3,000 mg a day. So read labels and choose wisely, keeping in mind the basic message for sodium is "eat less."

Our objective for the recipes in this book was to keep sodium low. Recognizing that most people require at least 1,800 calories, we rationalized that milligrams of sodium in most recipes needed to be less than the number of calories to keep sodium intake below 1,500 mg per day. Since even low-sodium versions of condiments like soy and fish sauces contain substantial amounts, several meals with strong Asian flavours did not make the cut. Cheese and cured meats were added as small flavourful morsels to limit the sodium content. And we discovered that even commercial breads could skyrocket levels. Fortunately no-salt-added versions of some products such as canned tomatoes and salmon are becoming generally available. For many recipes we suggest adding "salt and pepper to taste" giving you the option to add them or not. (Note that the nutrient analysis does not take into account any salt added "to taste.")

There is no need to lock the salt shaker away but use it with a light hand. And explore other means to jazz up your meals such as herbs, lemon juice and flavoured vinegars.

Nutrient Charts – The Facts

The "per serving" breakdown of key nutrients and the per cent Daily Value (%DV) in each main recipe or meal is included to provide information similar to that found on food labels. By definition, the DV for carbohydrate and fats is a benchmark for evaluating the amount a person eating a 2,000 calorie diet would need each day to have enough, and not too much. While ideally nutrients would be divided over the day with each meal providing about one third of the nutrients (33%DV), some meals will undoubtedly have more and others less. It all balances over several meals. (For more information see page 156).

There is no DV guideline for calories because energy needs vary greatly among individuals. And as we age, fewer calories are needed as most of us expend less energy at work and recreational activity, making weight gain a potential problem. Ultimately, the key to weight loss is a matter of increasing the calories used and/or reducing the calories eaten. But keep in mind that fewer calories must still provide all the nutrients that your body needs. So be sure to include a balance of foods from all the food groups. Just watch the portion size and enjoy being active.

Active Living

In addition to eating well, being active promotes better overall health and a sense of well-being. Canada's Physical Activity Guidelines recommend that adults accumulate at least 150 minutes of moderate to vigorous aerobic activity per week. So bike with your family, dance with your friends and ski or skate or swim. Build a daily walk or other activity into your daily routine. And check out the Health Canada website for activity guides and additional suggestions for active living.

An active lifestyle provides the foundation for independent living through more energy, good balance and stronger bones. Look for activities you enjoy — taking delight in what you do makes it easier to stick with it. When it comes to physical activity, the more you do the more benefit you reap.

Putting It All Together

Healthy living does not depend on any one food, food group or even a specific meal. Throughout these pages we highlight various aspects of eating well to illustrate that wise food selection following Canada's Food Guide really works. Eating well is based on the motto of variety, balance and moderation — the enjoyment of a variety of foods, with a good balance among food groups, eaten in moderation. Foods are to be savoured for their complementary flavours as well as their nutritive attributes. Simple, fine-flavoured meals that promote good health is what we've served up, here in *Fresh & Healthy Cooking for Two.*

MORNING STARTS

A good breakfast is more than just a cup of coffee or a glass of juice. Start your day off right with a breakfast routine that saves time and leaves you feeling energized. A bowl of fibre-rich cereal topped with fruit and milk brings the traditional combination of grains, fruit and dairy products together for a quick morning start. A handful of nuts rounds out the food groups, adding flavour and crunch. Introduce variety with different cereals and fruit. Or try a Fresh Fruit and Fibre Breakfast Smoothie (page 23) with any fruit you have on hand. If you go for toast, make it with whole grain bread and add a nutritious complement such as peanut butter or one of our more adventurous Toppings for Toast (page 27).

Planning ahead is also a time saver in the morning. Prepare some stewed fruit or make a batch of muffins on the weekend. Seedy Goodness Breakfast Cookies with Dried Fruit and Banana (page 32) are a perfect choice for a pick-up-and-run start to your day. They all go nicely with yogurt.

And for those special mornings when you have the time to sip your latte and read the paper, make it a breakfast with a difference. Try our Cranberry Pancakes with Oat Bran and Flax (page 28) or the Multi-Grain Waffles with Blueberry Compote (page 31) — two great ways to start the day!

Honey Almond Granola wi Shredded Coconut, Fresh Fru and Fibre Breakfast Smooth Best Banana Muffins, App Cinnamon Raisin Bran Muffin Carrot Muffins with Toaste Hazelnuts, Pumpkin Chocola Chip Muffins, Cranber Pancakes with Oat Bran and Fla Baked Apple Pancake, Mul Grain Waffles with Blueber Compote, Healthier Eg Benedict, Toppings for Toa Seedy Goodness Breakfa Cookies with Dried Fruit an Banana, Fruit and Nut Breakfa Bars Two-Oat Hot Cereal wi Flax, Honey Almond Granola wi Shredded Coconut, Fresh Fru and Fibre Breakfast Smooth Best Banana Muffins, App Cinnamon Raisin Bran Muffin Carrot Muffins with Toast Hazelnuts, Pumpkin Chocola Chip Muffins, Cranber Pancakes with Oat Bran and Fla Baked Apple Pancake, Mul Grain Waffles with Blueber Compote, Healthier Eg Benedict, Toppings for Toa Seedy Goodness Breakfa Cookies with Dried Fruit an Banana, Fruit and Nut Breakfa Bars Two-Oat Hot Cereal wi Flax, Honey Almond Granola wi Shredded Coconut, Fresh Fru and Fibre Breakfast Smooth Best Banana Muffins, App Cinnamon Raisin Bran Muffin Carrot Muffins with Toaste Hazelnuts, Pumpkin Chocola Chip Muffins, Cranber Pancakes with Oat Bran and Fla Baked Apple Pancake, Multi-Gra Waffles with Blueberry Compot Healthier Eggs Benedict, Toppin

Healthier Eggs Benedict 🎥

Preparation Time: 5 minutes Cook Time: 5 minutes

Eggs Benedict has been a popular breakfast dish since the late 1800s. The classic version uses a true Hollandaise made with butter and egg yolks. Our take is every bit as tasty and with a lot less fuss and calories. Add a thin slice of ham if you wish.

4 eggs
2 tbsp (25 mL) plain yogurt
1 tbsp (15 mL) mayonnaise
1/2 tbsp (7 mL) Dijon mustard
1 to 2 tsp (5 to 10 mL) fresh lemon
   juice
2 English muffins, halved and toasted
1 tsp (5 mL) butter

In a medium nonstick skillet, add water to a depth of 1 inch (2.5 cm) in the pan and bring to a gentle boil.

Break each egg into a small cup and slowly slide egg from cup into the water. Poach for 3 minutes or until eggs are cooked to desired firmness. With a slotted spoon, lift eggs onto a plate to drain.

Meanwhile, in a small bowl, combine yogurt, mayonnaise, mustard and lemon juice.

Place 2 muffin halves on each of two plates. Spread each half with 1/4 tsp (1 mL) butter and top with a poached egg. Spoon a quarter of the sauce over each egg.

Makes 2 servings.

Eggsense

Eggs have a lot to recommend them. A source of high-quality protein, eggs provide many important vitamins, minerals and a carotenoid, lutein, that plays a role in eye health. Eggs are magical for the cook. One egg yolk will emulsify 1/2 cup (125 mL) of oil to make a thick mayonnaise or thicken 1/3 cup (75 mL) milk for a custard. Egg white can also function as a thickener, but its unique function is the ability to incorporate air, a process that is the basis for meringues and foam cakes.

PER SERVING	
Amount	% Daily Value
Calories 340	
Fat 16g	25%
Saturated 5.0g	25%
Monounsaturated 6.6g	
Polyunsaturated 3.2g	
Sodium 480mg	20%
Carbohydrate 30g	10%
Fibre 2g	8%
Protein 18g	
Calcium 178mg	16%

Two-Oat Hot Cereal with Flax

Preparation Time: 1 minute Cook Time: 3 minutes

Plain old-fashioned oatmeal is still one of the healthiest foods around. Add a bit of oat bran and flax and you have a great food to start the day. If the mix is made ahead, preparing hot cereal in the microwave is almost as easy as pouring from a box. For a chewy texture, use large-flake oatmeal; for a smoother cereal, choose the quick-cooking kind. Adding dried fruit eliminates the need for sugar and provides extra fibre.

¼ cup (50 mL) Hot Cereal Mix (recipe below)
¾ cup (75 mL) water
Raisins, chopped dried apricots or other dried fruit as desired
Salt

In a large microwave-safe serving bowl, place Hot Cereal Mix and water. Add dried fruit and salt as desired.

   Microwave on 100% power for 1 ½ minutes and then 30% power for 1 ½ minutes. (For two servings, microwave on 100% power for 3 minutes and then 30% power for 3 minutes.) Times may vary depending on the microwave oven.

Makes 1 serving.

Hot Cereal Mix

4 cups (1 L) rolled oats
1 cup (250 mL) oat bran
½ cup (125 mL) ground flaxseed

In a large bowl, combine oats, oat bran and flaxseed. Transfer to a tightly covered container and store in the refrigerator for up to 1 month.

Makes 20 servings, about 5 cups (1.25 L).

PER SERVING	
Amount	**% Daily Value**
Calories 94	
Fat 3g	5%
Saturated 0.4g	2%
Monounsaturated 0.7g	
Polyunsaturated 14g	
Sodium 2mg	0%
Carbohydrate 15g	5%
Fibre 3g	12%
Protein 4g	
Calcium 24mg	

Honey Almond Granola with Shredded Coconut

Preparation Time: 5 minutes Cook Time: 10 minutes

Granola has become a popular morning dish, but commercial versions can be very high in calories and quite expensive. This version makes a delicious and nutritious toasted cereal in very short order.

4 cups (1 L) large-flake rolled oats
$^1/_3$ cup (75 mL) slivered almonds
$^1/_3$ cup (75 mL) wheat germ
$^1/_3$ cup (75 mL) shredded
  unsweetened coconut
$^1/_4$ tsp (1 mL) salt
$^1/_3$ cup (75 mL) liquid honey
3 tbsp (45 mL) canola oil

In a large microwave-safe bowl, combine oats, almonds, wheat germ, coconut and salt.

In a small measuring cup or bowl, whisk together honey and oil until well blended; stir into oatmeal mixture.

Microwave on 100% power for 3 minutes; stir then microwave for 2 minutes longer. Stir well and continue to microwave until mixture becomes slightly browned, stirring after each minute. Let stand until cool, stirring several times. Mixture will continue to brown while standing. Store in a tightly covered container for up to 1 month.

Makes 10 servings, $^1/_2$ cup (125 mL) each.

PER SERVING	
Amount	**% Daily Value**
Calories 249	
Fat 10g	15%
Saturated 2.6g	13%
Monounsaturated 4.3g	
Polyunsaturated 2.6g	
Sodium 62mg	3%
Carbohydrate 34g	11%
Fibre 4g	16%
Protein 7g	
Calcium 27mg	

Best Banana Muffins

Preparation Time: 15 minutes Cook Time: 20 minutes

Simple to make and irresistible to eat, this nutritious version of a popular muffin is a winner. Serve them with a side of yogurt for breakfast or with a cup of tea later in the day.

1 ½ cups (375 mL) all-purpose or part whole wheat flour

½ cup (125 mL) toasted wheat germ (instructions below)

⅓ cup (75 mL) lightly packed brown sugar

¼ cup (50 mL) chopped walnuts, pecans or other nuts, optional

2 tsp (10 mL) baking powder

½ tsp (2 mL) baking soda

½ tsp (2 mL) ground cinnamon

¼ tsp (1 mL) salt

1 egg

1 ½ cups (375 mL) mashed ripe banana, about 3 to 4 medium

¼ cup (50 mL) milk

¼ cup (50 mL) canola oil

Preheat oven to 375°F (190°C). In a large bowl, combine flour, wheat germ, brown sugar, nuts, baking powder, baking soda, cinnamon and salt.

In a small bowl, beat egg lightly; stir in banana, milk and oil. Add to dry ingredients, stirring just until moistened.

Spoon into nonstick or paper-lined muffin cups. Bake for 20 minutes or until tops are lightly browned and firm to the touch.

Makes 12 muffins.

PER SERVING (1 muffin)	
Amount	% Daily Value
Calories 171	
Fat 6	9%
Saturated 0.6g	3%
Monounsaturated 3.0g	
Polyunsaturated 1.8g	
Sodium 162mg	7%
Carbohydrate 27g	9%
Fibre 2g	8%
Protein 4g	
Calcium 20mg	2%

Wheat Germ

Wheat germ is one of our few good sources of vitamin E and also contains iron and some B vitamins. Toasting in a dry skillet enhances its nutty flavour. Enjoy it added to baked goods and meat loaves or sprinkled on cereal and yogurt. Because of its high content of polyunsaturated fat, it can become rancid quite rapidly and must be stored in the refrigerator.

Fresh Fruit and Fibre Breakfast Smoothie

Preparation Time: 5 minutes

Use your blender or food processor to whiz together a fresh and nutritious starter to the day. For a complete breakfast, enjoy this smoothie with any of our delicious muffins or toast. Smoothies are great as an addition to lunch or by themselves as a light snack and are a healthy choice as part of a meal on the go.

½ cup (125 mL) plain yogurt
¼ cup (50 mL) milk
¾ cup (175 mL) cubed ripe soft
  fruit such as banana, blueberries,
  cantaloupe, kiwifruit, mango,
  peaches, pears, pineapple,
  raspberries or strawberries
1 tbsp (15 mL) oat bran or 2 tbsp
  (25 mL) high-fibre cereal
Fruit jam or honey

If you use a blender, combine yogurt, milk, fruit, and oat bran; process until smooth. Add jam or honey to taste.

If you use a food processor, process yogurt, fruit and bran until smooth. Pour into a large glass. Stir in milk. Add jam or honey to taste.

Makes 1 serving, about 1 cup (250 mL).

PER SERVING	
Amount	**% Daily Value**
Calories 221	
Fat 4g	6%
Saturated 2.1g	11%
Monounsaturated 1.0g	
Polyunsaturated 0.4g	
Sodium 112mg	5%
Carbohydrate 41g	14%
Fibre 3g	12%
Protein 11g	
Calcium 304mg	28%

Pumpkin Chocolate Chip Muffins

Preparation Time: 10 minutes Cook Time: 20 minutes

Pumpkin and chocolate make exceptional partners for a simple but memorable muffin. For an even greater chocolate treat, stir in some extra chips.

1 ½ cups (375 mL) whole wheat flour
½ cup (125 mL) lightly packed brown sugar
1 tbsp (15 mL) baking powder
½ tsp (2 mL) ground cinnamon
½ tsp (2 mL) salt
¼ tsp (1 mL) grated nutmeg
½ cup (125 mL) mini chocolate chips
1 egg
¾ cup (175 mL) milk
½ cup (125 mL) cooked or canned pumpkin
¼ cup (50 mL) canola oil

Preheat oven to 400°F (200°C). In a large bowl, combine flour, brown sugar, baking powder, cinnamon, salt and nutmeg. Stir in chips.

In a medium bowl, combine egg, milk, pumpkin and oil. Add to flour mixture; stir until moistened, being careful not to overmix.

Spoon into nonstick or paper-lined muffin cups. Bake for 20 minutes or until tops are lightly browned and firm to the touch. Allow to cool in pan for 2 to 3 minutes, then loosen edges and turn out.

Makes 12 muffins.

Chocolate Benefits?

Does chocolate really have health benefits? While many of us chocolate lovers would like to think so, the answer is not so simple. The healthful compounds in chocolate are phytochemicals called flavonoids. Found also in fruit and vegetables, red wine, tea and cocoa powder, these substances may help to lower blood pressure, reduce blood cholesterol and benefit the heart in other ways. But most chocolate products contain very few flavonoids. Since cocoa powder is bitter and unpalatable, it is generally mixed with sugar, saturated fat and other additives, thereby diluting its benefits. Cocoa may also be treated with an alkali (Dutch process), which produces a milder flavour, but also destroys many of the phytochemicals. So enjoy chocolate as an occasional treat, choosing dark chocolate with a high cocoa content. Better yet, use fat-free "non-Dutch" cocoa powder.

PER SERVING (1 muffin)	
Amount	% Daily Value
Calories 188	
Fat 8g	12%
Saturated 2.4g	12%
Monounsaturated 3.9g	
Polyunsaturated 1.6g	
Sodium 180mg	8%
Carbohydrate 27g	9%
Fibre 2g	8%
Protein 4g	
Calcium 68mg	6%

Carrot Muffins with Toasted Hazelnuts

Preparation Time: 15 minutes Cook Time: 25 minutes.

Toasted hazelnuts add excellent flavour to these moist, nutritious muffins. No hazelnuts? Use any nut you happen to have on hand.

1 cup (250 mL) all-purpose flour

3/4 cup (175 mL) whole wheat flour

3/4 cup (175 mL) lightly packed brown sugar

1 tsp (5 mL) ground cinnamon

1 tsp (5 mL) baking powder

1 tsp (5 mL) baking soda

1/2 tsp (2 mL) grated nutmeg

1/4 tsp (1 mL) salt

1 egg

1 cup (250 mL) applesauce

2 tbsp (25 mL) canola oil

2 cups (500 mL) grated carrot

1/3 cup (75 mL) chopped toasted hazelnuts or other nuts (instructions below)

Preheat oven to 375°F (190°C). In a large bowl, combine all-purpose flour, whole wheat flour, brown sugar, cinnamon, baking powder, baking soda, nutmeg and salt.

In a medium bowl, whisk egg, applesauce and oil until blended. Add to flour mixture along with carrot and hazelnuts. Stir until blended.

Spoon into nonstick or paper-lined muffin cups. Bake for 25 minutes or until tops are lightly browned and firm to the touch. Allow to cool in pan for 2 to 3 minutes, then loosen edges and turn out.

Makes 12 muffins.

To Toast Nuts

Place chopped nuts in a dry skillet and heat over medium low until slightly browned, stirring frequently. Toasting time will vary depending on the size of the nut pieces, the type of pan and the heat level.

PER SERVING (1 muffin)	
Amount	**% Daily Value**
Calories 186	
Fat 5g	8%
Saturated 0.5g	3%
Monounsaturated 3.2g	
Polyunsaturated 1.1g	
Sodium 191mg	8%
Carbohydrate 33g	11%
Fibre 2g	8%
Protein 3g	
Calcium 31mg	3%

Toppings for Toast

When you crave an easy start to the day, a couple of slices of toast with a flavourful topping may be just what you need. Here are our suggestions; you may think of others. Serve with a piece of fresh fruit or glass of juice along with a tall glass of milk or some yogurt.

Toast a piece of your favourite bread and serve with one of the following toppings:

A bit of grainy mustard and slices of hard-cooked egg.

A slice or 2 of cold smoked turkey and a dollop of cranberry sauce or light mayonnaise.

A spread of almond butter and slices of banana.

Your favourite cheese or cheese spread and a slice of tomato. Place under broiler or in a toaster oven for a few minutes to melt the cheese.

Cottage cheese and a sprinkle of sliced green onion, poppy seeds or canned pineapple tidbits.

A slice of leftover beef roast and a bit of horseradish.

A layer of hummus (page 40) sprinkled with sesame seeds.

Several pieces of kippered herring.

A thin spread of peanut butter topped with a tasty jam or marmalade.

Kippers

Kippered herring, often called kippers, have been split and then cured by salting, drying and cold-smoking. They bring good amounts of omega-3 fatty acids.

Cranberry Pancakes with Oat Bran and Flax

Preparation Time: 10 minutes Cook Time: 10 minutes

These easy-to-make pancakes are a favourite Sunday-morning breakfast. Try different dried fruit such as apricots, blueberries or chopped apple to give a variety of flavours. Serve with a side of applesauce for added interest.

1/2 cup (125 mL) whole wheat flour
1/4 cup (50 mL) oat bran
2 tbsp (25 mL) ground flaxseed
1 tbsp (15 mL) lightly packed brown sugar
1 1/2 tsp (7 mL) baking powder
1 tsp (5 mL) ground cinnamon
1 egg
3/4 cup (175 mL) milk
1 tbsp (15 mL) canola oil
1/3 cup (75 mL) finely chopped dried cranberries or other dried fruit
1/4 cup (50 mL) maple syrup

In a large bowl, stir together flour, bran, flaxseed, brown sugar, baking powder and cinnamon.

In a small bowl, combine egg, milk and oil. Add to dry ingredients and fold in cranberries. Let stand for 2 minutes.

Heat a large nonstick skillet over medium-high heat. Drop small spoonfuls of batter onto skillet; cook until small bubbles form on the surface and the underside is golden brown. Turn pancakes and cook until the second side is lightly browned.

Serve pancakes with a drizzle of syrup.

Makes 2 servings of 5 small pancakes each.

Speaking to Your Heart

Oat bran, along with all oat products, is rich in beta glucan, a component of soluble fibre. Soluble fibre seems not only to play a role in lowering blood cholesterol, but may also help control blood sugar. Flaxseed also brings many nutritional benefits including omega-3 fatty acids, fibre and cancer-fighting lignans.

PER SERVING	
Amount	**% Daily Value**
Calories 481	
Fat 17g	26%
Saturated 3.0g	15%
Monounsaturated 6.6g	
Polyunsaturated 5.2g	
Sodium 335mg	14%
Carbohydrate 78g	26%
Fibre 9g	36%
Protein 14g	
Calcium 205mg	19%

Apple Cinnamon Raisin Bran Muffins

Preparation Time: 15 minutes Cook Time: 20 minutes

A favourite bran muffin with a double dose of apple. Add a smoothie (page 23) for a great way to start the day.

1 ½ cups (375 mL) whole wheat flour
¾ cup (175 mL) wheat bran
¼ cup (50 mL) lightly packed brown
  sugar
1 ½ tsp (7 mL) baking powder
1 tsp (5 mL) ground cinnamon
½ tsp (2 mL) baking soda
½ tsp (2 mL) salt
½ cup (125 mL) raisins
1 egg
½ cup (125 mL) milk
½ cup (125 mL) applesauce
¼ cup (50 mL) canola oil
3 tbsp (45 mL) molasses
1 cup (250 mL) finely chopped peeled
  apple

Preheat oven to 375°F (190°C). In a large bowl, combine flour, bran, brown sugar, baking powder, cinnamon, baking soda and salt. Stir in raisins.

In a medium bowl, whisk egg and stir in milk, applesauce, oil and molasses; stir in apple. Add egg mixture to flour mixture; stir until moistened being careful not to overmix.

Spoon into nonstick or paper-lined muffin cups. Bake for 20 minutes or until tops are lightly browned and firm to the touch. Allow to cool in pan for 2 to 3 minutes, then loosen edges and turn out.

Makes 12 muffins.

Muffins on Hand

For readily available muffins, store them in re-sealable bags in your freezer. To warm up, microwave a single muffin for 1 minute on your microwave's defrost setting.

PER SERVING (1 muffin)	
Amount	**% Daily Value**
Calories 190	
Fat 6g	9%
Saturated 0.7g	4%
Monounsaturated 3.0g	
Polyunsaturated 1.6g	
Sodium 198mg	8%
Carbohydrate 35g	12%
Fibre 4g	16%
Protein 4g	
Calcium 82mg	7%

Baked Apple Pancake

Preparation Time: 15 minutes Cook Time: 25 minutes

A variation of this pancake is a favourite of many Germanic-speaking peoples. Simple to prepare, it is delightful for a special Sunday-morning breakfast served hot from the oven with maple syrup.

1 tbsp (15 mL) butter
2 cups (500 mL) thinly sliced peeled firm tart apples
2 eggs
1/2 cup (125 mL) all-purpose flour
1/2 cup (125 mL) milk
1 tbsp (15 mL) granulated sugar
Pinch salt
1/2 tsp (2 mL) ground cinnamon or nutmeg
Pure maple syrup or icing sugar (optional)

Preheat oven to 425°F (220°C). Place butter in an 8-inch (2 L) square baking dish or a 9-inch (22 cm) ovenproof skillet. Place pan in oven until butter is melted, about 1 minute.

Add apples to pan, toss to coat evenly and bake for 5 minutes or until apples are slightly soft.

Meanwhile, in a small bowl, whisk eggs, flour, milk, sugar and salt until blended. Pour over apples; sprinkle with cinnamon or nutmeg. Bake for 20 minutes or until puffed and slightly browned on top. Cut into wedges and serve warm with maple syrup or icing sugar if desired.

Makes 2 servings.

PER SERVING	
Amount	% Daily Value
Calories 420	
Fat 13g	20%
Saturated 6.1g	31%
Monounsaturated 4.0g	
Polyunsaturated 1.3g	
Sodium 151mg	6%
Carbohydrate 66g	22%
Fibre 3g	12%
Protein 12g	
Calcium 120mg	11%

Multi-Grain Waffles with Blueberry Compote

Preparation Time: 10 minutes Cook Time: 15 minutes

Fragrant pancakes or waffles topped with a blueberry compote make an ideal way to celebrate a weekend breakfast. Grains in the form of oats, barley flour and wheat germ offer a pleasing nutty flavour packed with fibre and nutrients. Cook them either as waffles or on a grill for pancakes. They are also delicious served with pure maple syrup.

Compote:

1 cup (250 mL) frozen blueberries
1/4 cup (50 mL) pure maple syrup
1 tsp (5 mL) butter

Waffles:

3/4 cup (175 mL) barley flour
1/4 cup (50 mL) quick-cooking rolled oats
2 tbsp (25 mL) toasted wheat germ (see page 22 for toasting instructions)
1 tbsp (15 mL) granulated sugar
3/4 tsp (3 mL) baking powder
1/2 tsp (2 mL) ground cinnamon
1/4 tsp (1 mL) salt
3/4 cup (175 mL) milk
1 egg
1 tbsp (15 mL) canola oil

Compote:

In a microwave-safe container, combine blueberries, syrup and butter. Microwave on 100% power for 2 minutes, or just until blueberries are soft.

Waffles:

In a medium bowl, combine flour, oats, wheat germ, sugar, baking powder, cinnamon and salt.

In a small bowl, whisk together milk, egg and oil. Add to flour mixture and mix just until moistened.

Heat waffle iron until very hot. Spoon in enough batter to cover about 3/4 of the surface; cook until waffles are golden and crisp. Top with blueberry compote.

Pancakes:

Preheat a grill or large nonstick skillet until hot. Drop small spoonfuls of waffle batter onto skillet. Cook until the underside is golden brown; turn pancakes and cook until the second side is lightly browned.

Makes 2 servings of 2 waffles or 3 small pancakes each.

PER SERVING (1 waffle with 1/4 of the compote)	
Amount	% Daily Value
Calories 320	
Fat 9g	14%
Saturated 2.2g	11%
Monounsaturated 3.5g	
Polyunsaturated 2.1g	
Sodium 257mg	11%
Carbohydrate 53g	18%
Fibre 7g	28%
Protein 9g	
Calcium 94mg	9%

Barley Flour

Barley flour adds a nutty and appealing flavour to baked products. With less gluten than wheat, barley flour makes wonderful light quick breads and muffins. Use it to replace up to half of the wheat flour in yeast breads or all of the flour in other baked products.

Seedy Goodness Breakfast Cookies with Dried Fruit and Banana

Preparation Time: 20 minutes Cook Time: 20 minutes

Keep these delicious cookies on hand for those busy mornings when you need a quick breakfast on the go. Full of fibre and dried fruit, add a glass of milk and you have a fast and healthy start to your day.

1 cup (250 mL) quick-cooking rolled oats

³/₄ cup (175 mL) whole wheat flour

¹/₄ cup (50 mL) toasted wheat germ (see page 22 for toasting instructions)

¹/₄ cup (50 mL) oat bran

¹/₂ cup (125 mL) raisins

¹/₂ cup (125 mL) chopped dried apricots or dried cranberries

¹/₂ cup (125 mL) chopped dates

¹/₂ cup (125 mL) shelled sunflower seeds

2 cups (500 mL) mashed ripe banana, about 4 medium

¹/₃ cup (75 mL) canola oil

Preheat oven to 350°F (180°C). In a large bowl, mix together oats, flour, wheat germ, oat bran, raisins, apricots, dates and seeds.

In a small bowl, combine banana and oil. Stir into flour mixture.

Drop spoonfuls of batter onto lightly greased baking sheets about 2 inches (5 cm) apart; flatten with a fork. Bake for 20 minutes or until lightly browned. Remove cookies from sheets immediately and cool on a wire rack. Store in the refrigerator for up to a week or freeze for longer storage.

Makes 36 cookies.

Seedy Goodness

Seeds are small packages packed with good taste and nutrition. Along with B vitamins and minerals, these oil-rich kernels are a source of vitamin E. Although the fat in seeds is mostly unsaturated, which helps lower blood cholesterol levels, it also brings calories. So use seeds and nuts sparingly, sprinkling a tablespoonful on salads or adding to baking.

PER SERVING (1 cookie)	
Amount	**% Daily Value**
Calories 83	
Fat 4g	6%
Saturated 0.3g	2%
Monounsaturated 1.5g	
Polyunsaturated 1.4g	
Sodium 1mg	0%
Carbohydrate 13g	4%
Fibre 2g	8%
Protein 2g	
Calcium 8mg	1%

Fruit and Nut Breakfast Bars

Preparation Time: 15 minutes Cook Time: 40 minutes

These bars are perfect for tucking into a backpack or purse to enjoy as a mid-morning snack or to serve with afternoon tea. Filled with your choice of dried fruit and nuts, they offer a variety of nutrients to keep your energy level high.

1/2 cup (125 mL) lightly packed brown sugar
1/3 cup (75 mL) whole wheat flour
1/4 tsp (1 mL) baking soda
1/4 tsp (1 mL) salt
3 cups (750 mL) chopped dried fruit (apples, apricots, plums, peaches, cranberries)
1 1/4 cups (300 mL) chopped unsalted nuts (pecans, walnuts, almonds, hazelnuts)
2 eggs
1 tsp (5 mL) vanilla

Preheat 300°F (150°C). In a large bowl, combine brown sugar, flour, baking soda and salt. Chop fruit and nuts until the size of raisins. Add to brown sugar mixture and mix well.

In a small bowl, beat eggs and vanilla until thick and foamy. Stir into fruit mixture, mixing until all pieces are moistened. Press evenly into a greased 9-inch square (2 L) pan lined with parchment paper or foil. Bake for 40 minutes or until tops are firm and firm to the touch. Allow to cool in pan. Invert onto cutting board, peel off parchment and cut into bars.

Makes 12 bars.

PER SERVING	
Amount	**% Daily Value**
Calories 239	
Fat 8g	12%
Saturated 1.3g	7%
Monounsaturated 4.8g	
Polyunsaturated 1.7g	
Sodium 96mg	4%
Carbohydrate 40g	13%
Fibre 4g	16%
Protein 5g	
Calcium 36mg	3%

LUNCH & SUPPER FIXINGS

Nowhere is the midday pause so well honoured as around the Mediterranean. It should therefore come as no surprise that we have drawn inspiration from this region for our lunch and light-supper suggestions with tomatoes, olives, feta and fresh herbs enhancing many of our recipes. Favourites such as hummus and pasta salad have been revived along with some interesting fixings for potatoes. All are designed to be assembled with very little effort and time.

It is important that lunch and supper include adequate energy as well as items from all food groups. These recipes provide the core of the meal, but are not meant to stand alone. To complete the plate, a few ideas for Lunch Complements to round out the meal are suggested. Several carrot sticks and broccoli florets, a glass of milk and a fresh fruit can add much to a traditional sandwich. Give a lift to your sandwich with some whole grain bread, complement the filling with crispy greens and be prudent with the mayonnaise

Nutritional shortcomings are common at lunch, a moment often neglected in our hurried world. Lack of time and fast-food excesses are the main pitfalls. But the small salad or the instant soup coupled with coffee and a few cookies is bound to leave you wanting for energy by mid-afternoon and will do little to provide you with health-promoting nutrients. So be inspired by these recipes; then savour your lunch listening to your favourite music, enjoying the sun in your garden or simply relaxing with a friend before resuming the afternoon activities. At home, at the office or on the road, a good lunch is well within your reach.

Tabbouleh with Feta and Grape Tomatoes 🎥

Preparation Time: 15 minutes

It's not traditional, but feta cheese and a bit of balsamic vinegar add superior flavour to this popular Middle Eastern salad. Be sure to use fresh lemon juice. And if you have it available, sprinkle the finished salad with a bit of chopped fresh mint.

½ cup (125 mL) bulgur
Pinch salt
¾ cup (175 mL) boiling water
1 small clove garlic, minced
1 tbsp (15 mL) olive oil
1 tbsp (15 mL) fresh lemon juice
1 tsp (5 mL) balsamic vinegar
2 cups (500 mL) halved grape
   tomatoes or 2 large tomatoes, diced
1 green onion, chopped

¾ cup (175 mL) chopped fresh parsley
¼ cup (50 mL) crumbled feta cheese

In a medium bowl, place bulgur and salt; cover with boiling water. Let stand for 12 minutes. Fluff with a fork.

In a small bowl or jar with tight-fitting lid, whisk or shake together garlic, oil, lemon juice and vinegar. Toss with bulgur.

Mix in tomatoes, onion, parsley and cheese. Serve immediately or chill until serving time.

Makes 2 servings.

Variation: Tabbouleh with Quinoa

Replace bulgur with quinoa and increase water to 1 cup (250 mL). Place quinoa, salt and water in a small pan; bring to a boil, reduce heat, cover and boil gently for 12 minutes or until liquid is almost absorbed. Remove from heat, fluff with a fork and let rest until water is absorbed, about 10 minutes. Continue with instructions above.

⋆ Lunch Complements
Pita bread triangles
Hard-cooked egg slices

Starring Quinoa

A small seed from South America, quinoa was a staple of the ancient Incas. Prized for the high quality of its protein, quinoa cooks quickly, expanding to about three times its original volume. Use it to replace rice, couscous or bulgur.

PER SERVING	
Amount	**% Daily Value**
Calories 264	
Fat 12g	18%
Saturated 3.9g	20%
Monounsaturated 6.1g	
Polyunsaturated 1.0g	
Sodium 231mg	10%
Carbohydrate 35g	12%
Fibre 6g	24%
Protein 9g	
Calcium 127mg	12%

POTATOES AND THREE TOPPINGS 📹

Preparation and Cook Time: 10 minutes

Think "P" for Potatoes and for Potassium. One of the key benefits associated with vegetables and fruit is their potassium content and potatoes are among the best sources. Dress up potatoes with a variety of toppings. Just a few minutes in the microwave and they are ready for a tasty lunch.

Potatoes

2 large baking potatoes, about 6 oz
   (170 g) each
Canola oil for rubbing

Wash and dry potatoes. Using your hands, rub a thin coating of oil over potatoes. Microwave on 100% power for 6 minutes or until soft. Let stand 2 minutes.

Split potatoes in half and place on serving plates. With a fork, fluff the potato slightly. Spoon a quarter of a topping (recipes below) onto each half potato.

Makes 2 servings.

Ham and Leek Topping

1 tsp (5 mL) butter
1 small leek, white and light green
   parts only, chopped, or $1/3$ cup
   (75 mL) chopped onion
$1/4$ cup (50 mL) chopped ham
$3/4$ cup (175 mL) plain yogurt
2 tsp (10 mL) Dijon mustard
2 tsp (10 mL) prepared horseradish
Ground black pepper

In a small nonstick skillet, heat butter over medium heat. Add leek; cook for 3 minutes or until soft. Stir in ham, yogurt, mustard, horseradish and pepper to taste. Heat through but do not boil.

Broccoli Cheddar Topping

$3/4$ cup (175 mL) chopped broccoli
1 small onion, chopped
$3/4$ cup (175 mL) plain yogurt
Salt and ground black pepper
2 tbsp (25 mL) shredded Cheddar
   cheese

In a small covered microwave-safe dish, microwave broccoli and onion on 100% power for 1 minute or until slightly soft.

Stir in yogurt and salt and pepper to taste. Sprinkle half the cheese over the broccoli topping on each filled potato.

Tuna and Red Pepper Topping

$1/4$ cup (50 mL) chopped sweet red
   pepper
$1/2$ can (6 oz/170 g) water-packed
   tuna, drained and flaked
$3/4$ cup (175 mL) plain yogurt
1 tbsp (15 mL) mayonnaise
$1/4$ tsp (1 mL) curry powder
Salt and ground black pepper

In a small microwave-safe dish, microwave red pepper and tuna on 100% power for 1 minute or just until hot. Stir in yogurt, mayonnaise and curry powder. Add salt and black pepper to taste.

* Lunch Complements
Salad of greens with slices of avocado
Crisp apple

POTATOES WITH HAM LEEK TOPPING		
PER SERVING		
Amount		**% Daily Value**
Calories 279		
Fat 6g		9%
Saturated 2.6g		13%
Monounsaturated 2.1g		
Polyunsaturated 0.7g		
Sodium 334mg		14%
Carbohydrate 45g		15%
Fibre 4g		16%
Protein 12g		
Calcium 229mg		21%

POTATOES WITH BROCCOLI CHEDDAR TOPPING		
PER SERVING		
Amount		**% Daily Value**
Calories 272		
Fat 6g		9%
Saturated 2.6g		13%
Monounsaturated 1.8g		
Polyunsaturated 0.7g		
Sodium 150mg		6%
Carbohydrate 46g		15%
Fibre 5g		20%
Protein 13g		
Calcium 290mg		26%

POTATOES WITH TUNA AND RED PEPPER TOPPING		
PER SERVING		
Amount		**% Daily Value**
Calories 270		
Fat 6g		9%
Saturated 1.5g		8%
Monounsaturated 3.1g		
Polyunsaturated 1.8g		
Sodium 229mg		10%
Carbohydrate 40g		13%
Fibre 3g		12%
Protein 16g		
Calcium 195mg		18%

Hummus in Pita Pockets

Preparation Time: 10 minutes

Fibre-rich and full of flavour, hummus is perfect to keep on hand for quick snacks. Stuff it in pita breads to make a savoury sandwich, or serve it as a dip with tortilla dippers or fresh veggies. Add a bit of roasted red pepper for a touch of colour.

1 can (19 oz/540 mL) chickpeas or white kidney beans, drained and rinsed
2 cloves garlic
3 tbsp (45 mL) toasted sesame seeds (instructions below) or tahini
2 tbsp (25 mL) fresh lemon juice
2 tbsp (25 mL) olive oil
1 tbsp (15 mL) water
$1/2$ tsp (2 mL) ground cumin
$1/4$ tsp (1 mL) hot pepper sauce (optional)
2 tbsp (25 mL) chopped fresh parsley or 2 tsp (10 mL) dried
Salt and ground black pepper
2 pita breads (about 6 in/15 cm diameter)
2 leaves lettuce

In a food processor or blender, process chickpeas, garlic, sesame seeds, lemon juice, oil, water, cumin and hot sauce until very smooth. Add parsley and a bit more water if needed to give a smooth consistency. Process until mixed; add salt and pepper to taste.

Cut pitas in half. Using a knife, separate each half to form a pocket. Spoon about $1/4$ cup (50 mL) hummus into each half and tuck a piece of lettuce leaf on top. Store remaining hummus in a covered container in the refrigerator for up to one week.

Makes 2 servings with pita, and 1 cup (250 mL) hummus left for another use.

⋆ Lunch Complements
Quick Savoy Coleslaw (page 60)
Fresh mango slices

Attention All Women

Folate and iron, two nutrients that are often in short supply in women's diets, are plentiful in this hummus.

To Toast Sesame Seeds

Place seeds in a small microwave-safe dish and microwave on 100% power for about 3 minutes, stirring frequently, or toast in a dry skillet over medium heat until slightly browned.

PER SERVING	
Amount	% Daily Value
Calories 405	
Fat 13g	20%
Saturated 1.7g	9%
Monounsaturated 6.8g	
Polyunsaturated 3.3g	
Sodium 523mg	22%
Carbohydrate 59g	20%
Fibre 6g	24%
Protein 14g	
Calcium 167mg	15%

Curried Chicken Salad on Pita

Preparation Time: 10 minutes

Transform leftover chicken or turkey into a tasty filling to tuck into split pita breads, or use chopped turkey slices from the deli. Serve with strips of sweet red pepper as a colourful garnish.

1 tbsp (15 mL) light mayonnaise
2 tbsp (25 mL) plain yogurt
1/2 tsp (2 mL) curry powder
2/3 cup (150 mL) finely chopped
    cooked chicken or turkey, about
    3 oz (80 g)
3 green onions, thinly sliced
Salt and ground black pepper
4 leaves romaine lettuce, thinly sliced
2 pita breads (about 6 in/15 cm
    diameter)

In a small bowl, stir together mayonnaise, yogurt and curry powder. Mix in chicken, onions and salt and pepper to taste.

Cut pitas in half. Using a knife, separate each half to form a pocket. Place a quarter of the lettuce into each pita half and top with a quarter of the chicken mixture.

Makes 2 servings.

* Lunch Complements
Fresh pineapple wedges

PER SERVING	
Amount	% Daily Value
Calories 363	
Fat 10g	15%
Saturated 2.3g	12%
Monounsaturated 2.2g	
Polyunsaturated 1.7g	
Sodium 459mg	19%
Carbohydrate 38g	13%
Fibre 2g	8%
Protein 30g	
Calcium 118mg	11%

Curry Powder

Curry powder as sold in North America is a mixture of up to twenty finely ground spices. Some of the most commonly used are cardamom, chilies, cinnamon, cloves, coriander, cumin, fennel seed, fenugreek, mace, nutmeg, black pepper and turmeric. Since curry powder quickly loses its pungency, it should be stored in a cool place for no longer than two months.

Mixed Mushroom Panini with Sweet Onion and Emmenthal Cheese

Preparation Time: 5 minutes Cook Time: 15 minutes

A toasted cheese sandwich enhanced with a variety of mushrooms makes a warm lunch for a cold day. If you have a panini press, assemble the untoasted sandwich and grill until heated through.

2 panini buns, cut in half
1 tbsp (15 mL) light mayonnaise
1 tsp (5 mL) Dijon mustard
1 tbsp (15 mL) olive oil
2 cups (500 mL) sliced mixed
   mushrooms (white, crimini,
   stemmed shiitake),
   about 5 oz (150 g)
1 1/2 tsp (7 mL) chopped fresh thyme
   or 1/2 tsp (2 mL) dried
4 thin slices sweet onion
2 thin slices Emmenthal or provolone
   cheese

Preheat broiler and move racks to about 4 inches (10 cm) from heat. On a baking sheet, place buns cut side up. Place under preheated broiler for 2 minutes or until lightly toasted. Set aside.

In a small bowl, stir together mayonnaise and mustard. Set aside.

In a medium skillet, heat oil over medium heat. Add mushrooms and cook for 7 minutes or until mushrooms are soft and the liquid from the mushrooms has evaporated. Sprinkle with thyme.

Spread the bottom half of each bun with half the mayonnaise mixture. Top each with half the mushrooms, 2 onion slices and a slice of cheese. Place under broiler, for 1 to 2 minutes or until cheese is melted. Place bun tops over each sandwich.

Makes 2 servings.

★ Lunch Complements
Rutabaga sticks
Orange sections

Panino and Panini

Panino is the Italian word for a small bread roll and generally means a sandwich made from a small loaf of bread such as a ciabatta. Panini is the plural of panino, but it has come to be used by English speakers to mean a single grilled sandwich. No matter what you call it, it's a delicious and versatile lunch option.

PER SERVING

Amount	% Daily Value
Calories 344	
Fat 20g	31%
Saturated 6.9g	35%
Monounsaturated 7.5g	
Polyunsaturated 2.1g	
Sodium 340mg	14%
Carbohydrate 29g	10%
Fibre 2g	8%
Protein 14g	
Calcium 294mg	27%

Lunch Salad Triad 🎥

Preparation Time: 15 minutes Cook Time: 10 minutes

Three tasty salads arranged on lettuce make an attractive presentation for a simple lunch. With leftover chicken, most of the preparation can be done while the potatoes steam.

8 oz (250 g) small new potatoes, cut into 1/2-inch (2 cm) pieces

2 tbsp (25 mL) dry white wine

3 tsp (15 mL) extra-virgin olive oil, divided

Salt and ground black pepper

2 tbsp (25 mL) grated Parmesan cheese

2 tsp (10 mL) fresh lemon juice, divided

3/4 cup (175 mL) diced cooked chicken or turkey

1/2 cup (125 mL) chopped cucumber or thinly sliced celery

1 tbsp (15 mL) chopped, toasted walnuts (see page 26 for toasting instructions)

1 cup (250 mL) halved cherry tomatoes

1 tbsp (15 mL) chopped Kalamata olives

2 tbsp (25 mL) chopped fresh parsley

2 leaves romaine lettuce

In a medium saucepan, steam potatoes for 10 minutes or until tender. Transfer to a bowl. Drizzle the wine and 1 tsp (5 mL) olive oil over the potatoes. Mix well and add salt and pepper to taste.

In a second bowl, combine cheese, 1 tsp (5 mL) olive oil and 1 tsp (5 mL) lemon juice. Mix in chicken, cucumber and walnuts; add salt and pepper to taste.

In a third bowl, combine 1 tsp (5 mL) olive oil and 1 tsp (5 mL) lemon juice. Stir in tomatoes, olives, parsley, and salt and pepper to taste.

Line each of two plates with lettuce. Place half potato salad, half chicken salad and half tomato salad in separate mounds on top of lettuce.

Makes 2 servings.

✳ Lunch Complements
Carrot Muffins with Toasted Hazelnuts (page 26)
Wedges of fresh pineapple

No Leftover Chicken?

Place a boneless, skinless chicken breast on a microwave-safe plate. Cover loosely with wax paper and microwave on 50% power for 3 minutes or until chicken is cooked. Let cool and cut up for salad.

Carotene Boost

Both parsley and romaine lettuce offer significant amounts of carotene, a family of helpful antioxidants. Beta carotene, the best-known family member, can be converted by your body to vitamin A.

PER SERVING

Amount	% Daily Value
Calories 460	
Fat 21g	32%
Saturated 4.1g	21%
Monounsaturated 9.3g	
Polyunsaturated 5.2g	
Sodium 224mg	9%
Carbohydrate 34g	11%
Fibre 5g	20%
Protein 34g	
Calcium 124mg	11%

Dijon-Maple Grilled Chicken with Fresh Spring Salad

Preparation Time: 15 minutes Cook Time: 10 minutes

This salad is perfect for lunch outside on a warm summer day. Enjoy some fruit punch with cheese and crackers while the chicken grills on the barbeque. Double or triple the recipe for extra guests.

Salad:
4 cups (1 L) mixed greens (mesclun, romaine, red leaf lettuce)
¼ seedless cucumber, unpeeled and sliced thinly
½ cup (125 mL) halved cherry or grape tomatoes

Dressing:
2 tbsp (25 mL) olive oil
1 ½ tbsp (22 mL) red wine vinegar
2 tsp (10 mL) finely grated fresh ginger
1 tsp (5 mL) Dijon mustard
½ tsp (2 mL) honey

Chicken:
2 tbsp (25 mL) Dijon mustard
1 tbsp (15 mL) maple syrup
1 large boneless, skinless chicken breast, about 8 oz (250 g)

Salad:
In a large bowl, combine greens, cucumber and tomatoes.

Dressing:
In a small bowl, whisk together oil, vinegar, ginger, mustard and honey.

Chicken:
In a second small bowl, combine mustard and maple syrup.

Brush chicken breast with mustard-maple mixture and cook over hot grill for 5 minutes; turn breast over, brush with more mustard mixture and cook for 5 minutes longer or until centre is no longer pink.

When ready to serve, pour dressing over greens and toss to mix. Divide salad onto two serving plates. Cut chicken into thin strips and arrange over greens.

Makes 2 servings.

* Lunch Complements
Cream of Carrot Soup (page 128) with rye crackers.
Whole grain roll

Mesclun

Mesclun is a mixture of small, young salad leaves, such as lettuces, arugula, spinach, Swiss chard, endive, mustard greens, dandelion, radicchio and beet greens. Give it a quick rinse and spin dry before using. In a plastic bag in the refrigerator, it will keep up to five days.

PER SERVING	
Amount	**% Daily Value**
Calories 314	
Fat 16g	25%
Saturated 2.3g	12%
Monounsaturated 10.7g	
Polyunsaturated 1.7g	
Sodium 98mg	4%
Carbohydrate 17g	6%
Fibre 2g	8%
Protein 27g	
Calcium 50mg	5%

Mini-Frittata with Ham, Sweet Red Pepper and Plum Tomato

Preparation Time: 10 minutes Cook Time: 15 minutes

Frittata is the Italian version of an omelet. The filling ingredients are mixed with the egg and it is served open-faced, making for simple preparation. Although traditionally finished under the broiler, it is equally happy baking in a hot oven. Almost anything can be added — chopped spinach, broccoli, kale, mushrooms, potatoes, fresh herbs. Be creative!

¼ cup (50 mL) chopped ham,
  kielbasa or pepperoni sausage
1 to 2 green onions, finely chopped
¼ cup (50 mL) chopped sweet red
  pepper
4 large eggs
¼ cup (50 mL) milk
Salt and ground black pepper
¼ cup (50 mL) shredded mozzarella,
  Monterey Jack or other cheese
2 plum tomatoes, thinly sliced

Preheat broiler (if using oven, preheat at 350°F (180°C)). Meanwhile, in a small nonstick skillet, cook ham over medium heat for 3 minutes or until hot. Distribute evenly in pan and scatter onions and red pepper over top.

In a small bowl, whisk eggs with milk and salt and pepper as desired. Pour over ham mixture; sprinkle cheese over top and arrange tomato slices over cheese.

Cook over medium-low heat for 6 minutes or until egg is almost set in the centre, then place under broiler for 2 to 3 minutes to finish cooking. Alternatively, the frittata can be baked in an oven for 20 minutes or until set in the centre.

Loosen frittata all around with a rubber spatula to remove from pan; slide onto a serving plate.

Makes 2 servings.

* Lunch Complements
Slices of crusty whole-grain loaf
Small green salad

PER SERVING	
Amount	% Daily Value
Calories 260	
Fat 15g	23%
Saturated 5.7g	29%
Monounsaturated 5.5g	
Polyunsaturated 1.8g	
Sodium 384mg	16%
Carbohydrate 11g	4%
Fibre 2g	8%
Protein 20g	
Calcium 176mg	16%

Watch the Fat

Ham is a good choice if you are watching calories as it is relatively low in fat. Kielbasa and other spicy sausage add great flavour, but bring higher amounts of fat.

Warm Pasta Salad with Shrimp, Olives and Feta 📹

Preparation Time: 15 minutes Cook Time: 10 minutes

This colourful salad is festive enough for a special luncheon or simple enough for a quick small meal. Whole wheat pasta is a flavourful alternative to pasta made from white flour. Another time, replace the shrimp with a can of flaked tuna.

Dressing:

2 tbsp (25 mL) extra-virgin olive oil
1 tbsp (15 mL) balsamic vinegar
1 clove garlic, minced
Salt and ground black pepper

Salad:

1 cup (250 mL) whole wheat fusilli or
  rotini pasta
1 large ripe tomato, chopped
1 cup (250 mL) cooked shrimp or
  1 can (6 oz/170 g) salad shrimp,
  drained
$1/3$ cup (75 mL) crumbled feta cheese
$1/4$ cup (50 mL) chopped pitted black
  olives such as Kalamata
$1/4$ cup (50 mL) chopped red onion
$1/4$ cup (50 mL) chopped fresh basil

Dressing:

In a small bowl, whisk together oil, vinegar, garlic and salt and pepper to taste. Set aside.

Salad:

In a large pot of boiling salted water, cook pasta for 10 minutes or until tender but firm. Drain and rinse in hot water.

In a medium bowl, combine tomato, shrimp, cheese, olives, onion, basil and warm pasta. Pour dressing over and toss gently to mix. Serve immediately.

Makes 2 servings.

⋆ Lunch Complements
Red and green grapes

Savouring the Olive

For centuries, olives have been grown for both their fruit and their high oil content. All fresh olives, whether green underripe olives or the black fully ripe fruit, are bitter. Olives are processed to remove the bitter substances in a variety of ways depending on the style of final product. Kalamata, a popular variety from the Kalamata region of Greece, is a large smooth black olive with a meaty texture.

PER SERVING	
Amount	**% Daily Value**
Calories 471	
Fat 22g	34%
Saturated 6.1g	31%
Monounsaturated 12.2g	
Polyunsaturated 2.1g	
Sodium 527mg	22%
Carbohydrate 46g	15%
Fibre 6g	24%
Protein 27g	
Calcium 196mg	18%

DINNER IS SERVED

As a time to pause and set aside the concerns of the day, the evening meal offers relaxation and the anticipation of enjoyment. For answers to the age-old question "What's for dinner?" we searched for delicious, nutritious and innovative solutions that require a minimum of preparation. Here, you will find updated traditional favourites such as burgers with a simple Chimichurri sauce in a two-serving size. Also we rediscovered edamame for making a tasty stir-fry and found some delicious and easy ways for dressing up convenient fish fillets.

Our dinners are served with suggestions for vegetable and starch accompaniments, accented with a variety of savoury flavourings to tempt the most capricious palates. These suggestions bring a remarkable payoff, often delivering a full complement of vitamins A and C and a good third of fibre needs while keeping fat and sodium levels in line. A basic nutritional analysis for both the main dish and the total dinner is provided. But one meal cannot do it all, no matter how balanced; a good dinner is just a complement to a healthy breakfast and lunch. If dinner is served with a bite to whet your appetite, a crusty roll or a dessert, select these elements wisely to balance the day's food choices as well as to enhance the enjoyment of the meal. This is fresh and healthy food in action.

Naturally we invite you to mix and match the suggestions for the "+" side dishes to round out the meal to accommodate your taste and what you have on hand. Be a bit adventurous and try some less familiar grains and vegetables such as bulgur, fennel or Swiss chard; we guarantee a pleasant surprise.

Three-Cheese Pasta Bake with Tomatoes and Spinach

Preparation Time: 10 minutes Cook Time: 40 minutes

Pasta forms a base to support a filling of spinach and a trio of cheese rich in calcium and vitamin A.

5 oz (150 g) small pasta (small shells, macaroni), about 1 1/4 cups (300 mL)

1 egg

1/4 cup (50 mL) grated Parmesan cheese

3 tbsp (45 mL) milk

Salt and ground black pepper

3 cups (750 mL) packed chopped fresh spinach

1/2 cup (125 mL) ricotta cheese

1/4 tsp (1 mL) ground nutmeg

2 to 3 plum tomatoes, cored and thinly sliced

1/4 cup (50 mL) shredded part-skim Mozzarella cheese

Preheat oven to 350°F (180°C). In a large pot of boiling, salted water, cook pasta for 8 to 10 minutes or until tender but firm. Drain.

Meanwhile, in a medium bowl, whisk together egg, Parmesan cheese and milk. Mix in pasta and salt and pepper if desired. Spread on bottom of a lightly greased 9 x 5-inch (2 L) baking pan.

Rinse spinach. Place in a glass measure or microwave-safe bowl. Cover with plastic wrap. Microwave on 100% power for 1 1/2 to 2 minutes or until spinach is just wilted. Drain spinach, pressing to remove liquid. Stir in ricotta cheese and nutmeg.

Spread spinach mixture over pasta. Arrange tomato slices on top and sprinkle with mozzarella. Bake uncovered for 30 minutes. Let stand for 5 minutes before serving.

Makes 2 servings.

PER SERVING OF MAIN DISH	
Amount	**% Daily Value**
Calories 550	
Fat 15g	23%
Saturated 7.9g	40%
Monounsaturated 4.5g	
Polyunsaturated 1.4g	
Sodium 417mg	17%
Carbohydrate 72g	24%
Fibre 5g	20%
Protein 31g	
Calcium 491mg	45%

+ Mixed Vegetable Salad

Raw veggies add extra crunch and fibre to a green salad.

2 tbsp (25 mL) light mayonnaise
1 tbsp (15 mL) salsa
1/4 tsp (1 mL) granulated sugar
2 cups (500 mL) assorted torn greens
1/2 cup (125 mL) shredded red
  cabbage
1/4 cup (50 mL) sliced cauliflower
  florets
1/4 cup (50 mL) sliced celery

In a small bowl, whisk together mayonnaise, salsa and sugar. Set aside.
   In a salad bowl, combine greens, cabbage, cauliflower and celery.
Toss with dressing.

PER SERVING WITH SIDE DISHES		
Amount		% Daily Value
Calories 628		
Fat 20g		31%
Saturated 8.1g		41%
Monounsaturated 6.7g		
Polyunsaturated 2.6g		
Sodium 612mg		26%
Carbohydrate 82g		27%
Fibre 8g		32%
Protein 33g		
Calcium 543mg		49%

Brazilian Beans and Rice

Preparation Time: 10 minutes Cook Time: 55 minutes

In Brazil, the combination of black beans and rice is eaten at least once a day, in the same way that bread is on the table in many other countries. A tasty and hearty dish, the complementary nature of these two foods provides a high quality protein making it is a good choice for vegetarians. An added bonus is lots of fibre and an amazing quantity of folate.

1 tsp (5 mL) canola oil
1 onion, chopped
1 clove garlic, minced
$\frac{1}{2}$ cup (125 mL) chopped green
    pepper
$\frac{1}{2}$ cup (125 mL) chopped celery
$\frac{3}{4}$ cup (175 mL) water
$\frac{1}{2}$ cup (125 mL) low-sodium chicken
    broth
$\frac{1}{4}$ cup (50 mL) tomato paste
$\frac{1}{4}$ cup (50 mL) brown rice
$\frac{1}{2}$ tsp (2 mL) chili powder
$\frac{1}{2}$ tsp (2 mL) ground cumin
2 cups (500 mL) cooked black beans
    or 1 can (19 oz/540 mL) black beans,
    drained and rinsed
Salt and ground black pepper
2 tbsp (25 mL) grated Parmesan
    cheese

In a large saucepan, heat oil over medium heat. Cook onions, garlic, green pepper and celery for 7 minutes or until very soft.

Add water, broth, tomato paste, rice, chili powder and cumin. Bring to a boil. Reduce heat, cover and simmer for 40 minutes or until rice is cooked.

Add beans and cook for 5 minutes or until hot. Add salt and pepper to taste. Serve sprinkled with cheese.

Makes 2 servings.

Variation: Lentils and Rice

Replace the beans with $\frac{1}{4}$ cup (50 mL) dried brown lentils, adding lentils at the same time as the rice.

PER SERVING OF MAIN DISH	
Amount	**% Daily Value**
Calories 445	
Fat 7g	11%
Saturated 1.8g	9%
Monounsaturated 2.2g	
Polyunsaturated 1.6g	
Sodium 180mg	8%
Carbohydrate 77g	26%
Fibre 17g	68%
Protein 24g	
Calcium 175mg	16%

+ Swiss Chard with Balsamic Vinegar

Swiss chard, with its dark green leaves, is high on the list of nutritious vegetables. Just a splash of vinegar cuts the slight bitterness and adds a delicious pungent flavour.

8 oz (250 g) Swiss chard, sliced
1 tbsp (15 ml) balsamic vinegar

Steam Swiss chard for about 5 to 8 minutes, or until tender. Drain. Place in a medium bowl and splash with balsamic vinegar.

PER SERVING WITH SIDE DISHES	
Amount	**% Daily Value**
Calories 594	
Fat 12g	18%
Saturated 2.7g	14%
Monounsaturated 6.4g	
Polyunsaturated 4.2g	
Sodium 553mg	23%
Carbohydrate 102g	34%
Fibre 21g	84%
Protein 27g	
Calcium 283mg	26%

+ Pineapple Carrot Salad with Creamy Dressing

An old-fashioned creamy dressing is perfect for a salad of sweet lettuces and carrot.

2 tbsp (25 mL) mayonnaise
1 tbsp (15 mL) granulated sugar
1 tbsp (15 mL) cider vinegar
1 tbsp (15 mL) milk
Salt and ground black pepper
3 cups (750 mL) assorted lettuces
1/4 cup (50 mL) pineapple tidbits
1/4 cup (50 mL) shredded carrot

In a small bowl, whisk together mayonnaise, sugar, vinegar, milk and salt and pepper to taste. Set aside.

In a salad bowl, combine lettuces, pineapple and carrot. Toss with dressing.

Fibre Bounty

There are an amazing 21 grams of fibre in this meal, almost a full day's minimum requirement, with most coming from the beans. Fibre has many health benefits, providing resistance training for the digestive tract muscles while moderating cholesterol and glucose levels. Remember to drink plenty of liquids and eat smaller portions if you are adjusting to meals with more fibre.

To Cook Beans

Canned beans are the ultimate in convenience. If you choose the longer and more economical route, you can also reduce the amount of sodium, which is high in canned beans. Cook a large amount of dried beans, freezing the leftovers in small containers to use another time.

Rinse dried beans. Place in a large saucepan and cover with cold water by 2 inches (5 cm). Bring to a boil. Reduce heat and boil gently for 2 minutes. Remove from heat and let stand for 1 hour. Or soak beans overnight in enough cold water to cover beans by 2 inches (5 cm). Drain beans and cover with fresh cold water. Bring to a boil. Reduce heat and simmer for 30 to 60 minutes or until beans are tender. Add a bit of salt during the last half of cooking time.

One cup (250 mL) dry beans yields about 2 1/2 cups (625 mL) cooked beans.

Baked Chicken with a Sesame Crust

Preparation Time: 5 minutes Cook Time: 40 minutes

Sesame seeds add a pleasing crunch to this popular yogurt-crumb coating for chicken.

⅓ cup (75 mL) fine dry bread crumbs
1 tbsp (15 mL) sesame seeds
⅓ cup (75 mL) yogurt
1 tbsp (15 mL) Dijon mustard
2 skinless chicken breast halves or
  legs, about 5 oz (140 g) each

Preheat oven to 375°F (190°C). In a shallow bowl, combine crumbs and seeds.

In a second shallow bowl, combine yogurt and mustard.

Dip chicken into mustard mixture, then roll in crumb mixture.

Place chicken in a flat baking dish. Bake, uncovered, for 40 to 50 minutes or until chicken is no longer pink in the centre.

Makes 2 servings.

+ Roasted Potatoes

Roast potatoes to a fragrant crispness alongside the chicken.

2 potatoes
1 tsp (5 mL) oil
1 ½ tsp (7 mL) chopped fresh thyme,
  or ½ tsp (2 mL) dried

Preheat oven to 375°F (190°C). Peel potatoes and cut each into 4 to 6 pieces. Place pieces in a small bowl. Add oil and thyme; mix well. Place potatoes on a baking sheet and roast for 30 minutes alongside the chicken.

PER SERVING OF MAIN DISH	
Amount	% Daily Value
Calories 245	
Fat 6g	9%
Saturated 1.3g	7%
Monounsaturated 1.9g	
Polyunsaturated 1.7g	
Sodium 227mg	9%
Carbohydrate 17g	6%
Fibre 1g	4%
Protein 30g	
Calcium 163mg	15%

+ Cabbage Toss

Toss a simple yogurt dressing with your choice of cabbage. Green and red are the most common types of cabbage. Savoy and napa have the mildest flavour and softest texture.

2 tbsp (25 mL) plain yogurt
1 tbsp (15 mL) light mayonnaise
1/4 tsp (1 mL) dried marjoram
1/4 tsp (1 mL) granulated sugar
1/4 tsp (1 mL) wine vinegar
Pinch of salt
2 cups (500 mL) finely sliced cabbage
1/4 cup (50 mL) chopped celery
1/4 cup (50 mL) chopped sweet red
  pepper

In a small bowl, whisk together yogurt, mayonnaise, marjoram, sugar, vinegar and salt. Set aside.

In a salad bowl, combine cabbage, celery and red pepper. Toss with dressing.

+ Carrots Provençale

The fruity flavour of black olives, a hint of garlic and olive oil transform ordinary carrots into a rewarding side dish.

8 oz (250 g) baby carrots
1/4 cup (50 mL) water
4 black olives, chopped
1 tsp (5 mL) olive oil
1 clove garlic, minced
Salt and ground black pepper

In a small saucepan, cook carrots in water for 6 to 7 minutes or until tender; drain. Add olives, olive oil, garlic and salt and pepper to taste; stir and heat through.

PER SERVING WITH SIDE DISHES	
Amount	% Daily Value
Calories 534	
Fat 14g	22%
Saturated 2.3g	12%
Monounsaturated 6.7g	
Polyunsaturated 4.0g	
Sodium 506mg	21%
Carbohydrate 68g	23%
Fibre 11g	44%
Protein 39g	
Calcium 396mg	36%

The Sesame Touch

A few sesame seeds add a unique flavour as well as valuable iron and fibre. Their fat content is not negligible, but most of it is the healthy unsaturated kind. Sesame oil is a staple ingredient in Asian cooking. Tahini, made from ground sesame seeds, is often called "butter of the Middle East."

Citrus Shrimp with Asian Noodles 📹

Preparation Time: 10 minutes Cook Time: 10 minutes

Sautéing seafood is one of the fastest ways to get dinner on the table. A hint of orange and lemon wonderfully enhances the succulent flavour of shrimp without overwhelming it.

1 tsp (5 mL) grated orange zest
1 tsp (5 mL) grated lemon zest
1/3 cup (75 mL) orange juice
2 tbsp (25 mL) fresh lemon juice
2 tsp (10 mL) olive oil
1/2 tsp (2 mL) finely grated fresh ginger
1/8 tsp (0.5 mL) salt
1 tsp (5 mL) canola oil
8 oz (250 g) fresh or uncooked frozen shelled shrimp, about 10 oz (280 g) with shells
5 oz (150 g) linguini-style rice noodles, cooked according to package instructions
1 tbsp (15 mL) chopped fresh parsley

In a small bowl, combine orange zest, lemon zest, orange juice, lemon juice, olive oil, ginger and salt. Set aside.

In a medium nonstick skillet, heat canola oil over medium-high heat. Add shrimp; cook for 4 minutes or until the shrimp turn pink. Add citrus mixture; bring just to a boil. Arrange shrimp over noodles and pour sauce over top. Sprinkle with parsley.

Makes 2 servings.

+ Quick Savoy Coleslaw 📹

A light coleslaw dressing that doesn't mask the flavour of sweet savoy cabbage.

1/2 clove garlic, minced
1 tbsp (15 mL) olive oil
1 tbsp (15 mL) white wine vinegar
1 tbsp (15 mL) water
2 tsp (10 mL) granulated sugar
1/2 tsp (2 mL) Dijon mustard
2 cups (500 mL) shredded savoy or other cabbage

In a medium bowl, whisk together garlic, olive oil, vinegar, water, sugar and mustard. Add cabbage and toss to mix.

+ Oriental Beans 📹

Just a splash of soy sauce adds flavour without fat. We use the sodium-reduced version for less salt.

1 1/2 cups (375 mL) whole green beans
1/4 cup (50 mL) water
1 clove garlic, minced
1 tsp (5 mL) sodium-reduced soy sauce

In a small saucepan, bring beans and water to a boil; reduce heat, cover and cook for 7 minutes or until tender but firm. Drain and toss with garlic and soy sauce.

PER SERVING OF MAIN DISH		PER SERVING WITH SIDE DISHES	
Amount	% Daily Value	Amount	% Daily Value
Calories 459		Calories 572	
Fat 9g	14%	Fat 16g	25%
Saturated 1.3g	7%	Saturated 2.2g	11%
Monounsaturated 5.1g		Monounsaturated 10.1g	
Polyunsaturated 1.9g		Polyunsaturated 2.5g	
Sodium 442mg	18%	Sodium 544mg	23%
Carbohydrate 66g	22%	Carbohydrate 78g	26%
Fibre 2g	8%	Fibre 5g	20%
Protein 26g		Protein 28g	
Calcium 81mg	7%	Calcium 124mg	11%

GRILLED CHICKEN THREE WAYS

Preparation Time: 5 minutes Cook Time: 15 minutes

A trio of simple sauces give interesting flavour to grilled boneless chicken breasts without the high amount of sodium found in most commercial barbecue sauces. Each sauce recipe will make enough for two chicken breasts.

Grilled Chicken with Blueberry-Orange Sauce

Blueberry and ambrosial marmalade bring wonderful flavour highlights to grilled chicken

1/2 cup (125 mL) fresh or frozen
   blueberries
2 tbsp (25 mL) orange marmalade
1/2 tsp (2 mL) water
2 boneless skinless chicken breasts,
   about 4 oz (125 g) each

In a 2-cup (500 mL) glass measure, combine blueberries, marmalade and water. Microwave on 100% power for 3 minutes or until boiling and slightly thickened.

Grill chicken over medium coals until no longer pink in the centre, about 6 minutes on each side. Place chicken on plates and spoon sauce over top.

Makes 2 servings.

+ Cabbage Apple Salad with Yogurt Dressing

Both apple and a dressing made with apple cider enhance a cabbage salad.

1/4 cup (50 mL) plain yogurt
1/4 cup (50 mL) apple cider or apple
   juice
1 tbsp (15 mL) chopped fresh parsley
1 tsp (5 mL) liquid honey
2 cups (500 mL) chopped savoy
   cabbage
1 apple, cored and chopped

In a small bowl, whisk together yogurt, cider, parsley and honey. Set aside.

In a salad bowl, combine cabbage and apple. Toss with dressing.

+ Potatoes in Foil

Potatoes cook in a foil package alongside the rest of the meal.

2 potatoes
1 onion, thinly sliced
2 tsp (5 mL) butter, melted

Slice potatoes thinly and tuck slices of onion in between the potato slices; place each potato with onion on a square of foil and drizzle each with half the butter. Seal foil tightly to make two small packets. Place packets over medium coals and cook for 20 minutes, turning frequently, or until potato is soft.

+ Grilled Asparagus

Simple is often best when enjoying asparagus in season.

½ lb (250 g) fresh asparagus
1 tsp (5 mL) olive oil

Place asparagus in a grill basket. Brush with olive oil and place over medium heat; grill for 3 to 5 minutes or until tender and slightly browned. Drizzle with extra olive oil before serving if desired.

PER SERVING OF MAIN DISH	
Amount	% Daily Value
Calories 193	
Fat 2g	3%
Saturated 0.4g	2%
Monounsaturated 0.3g	
Polyunsaturated 0.3g	
Sodium 84mg	4%
Carbohydrate 19g	6%
Fibre 1g	4%
Protein 26g	
Calcium 22mg	2%

To Peel or Not to Peel

Eat potatoes with their skins for a rich source of fibre and a higher nutrient concentration than you would get from peeled potatoes. But do remove the skin and underlying flesh if it has turned green. The green is chlorophyll, and while not harmful in itself, it may indicate the presence of a toxic alkaloid called solanine. In large amounts, solanine can cause digestive discomfort and fatigue.

PER SERVING WITH SIDE DISHES	
Amount	% Daily Value
Calories 499	
Fat 9g	14%
Saturated 3.6g	18%
Monounsaturated 3.3g	
Polyunsaturated 0.9g	
Sodium 165mg	7%
Carbohydrate 76g	25%
Fibre 9g	36%
Protein 34g	
Calcium 152mg	14%

Grilled Chicken with Chili Sauce

The tangy notes of chili and horseradish bring a pleasing lift to this barbeque favourite.

1/3 cup (75 mL) chili sauce
1 tsp (5 mL) cornstarch
1/2 tsp (2 mL) prepared horseradish
1 tbsp (15 mL) red wine vinegar
2 boneless skinless chicken breasts,
  about 4 oz (125 g) each

In a 2-cup (500 mL) glass measure, combine chili sauce, cornstarch and horseradish. Microwave on 100% power for 2 minutes or until boiling and slightly thickened, stirring once. Stir in vinegar.

Grill chicken over medium coals until no longer pink in the centre, about 6 minutes on each side. Place chicken on serving plates and top with sauce.

Makes 2 servings.

+ Grilled New Potatoes

Take advantage of potatoes while they are still new. For easy preparation, parboil potatoes and parsnips together in the same saucepan before grilling.

4 to 6 small new potatoes , whole,
  or larger ones cut in half
1 tsp (5 mL) canola oil

In a small pan of boiling water, parboil potatoes for 5 minutes; drain and let cool. Place potatoes in a small bowl and toss with canola oil. Place potatoes directly on a hot grill and cook over medium heat until soft, about 10 minutes.

+ Maple Roasted Parsnips

Grilling brings out the sweetness of parsnips, which is enhanced by a splash of maple syrup.

2 to 3 parsnips, peeled and sliced
  lengthwise
1 tsp (5 mL) canola oil
1 tbsp (15 mL) maple syrup

Preheat grill to hot, or oven to 450°F (230°C). In a small pan of boiling water, parboil parsnips for 5 minutes; drain and let cool. Toss with oil, coating evenly. Grill or bake for 15 minutes or until tender and browned, turning once. Place in a serving bowl and drizzle with maple syrup.

+ Tomato Avocado Summer Salad

Tomatoes and avocados make an unbeatable combination for a summer salad. Although avocados are high in fat, it is the heart-healthy monounsaturated kind.

1 tbsp (15 mL) olive oil
1 1/2 tsp (7 mL) balsamic vinegar
1/2 tsp (2 mL) red wine vinegar
2 cups halved cherry tomatoes
2 carrots, thinly sliced
1 avocado, cut into cubes
1/4 cup (50 mL) coarsely chopped
  sweet onion
6 leaves fresh basil, chopped

In a small bowl, whisk together olive oil, balsamic vinegar and red wine vinegar. Set aside.

In a salad bowl, combine tomatoes, carrots, avocado, onion and basil. Toss with dressing.

PER SERVING OF MAIN DISH	
Amount	% Daily Value
Calories 135	
Fat 2g	3%
Saturated 0.4g	2%
Monounsaturated 0.3g	
Polyunsaturated 0.3g	
Sodium 168mg	7%
Carbohydrate 3g	1%
Fibre 0g	0%
Protein 26g	
Calcium 22mg	2%

PER SERVING WITH SIDE DISHES	
Amount	% Daily Value
Calories 702	
Fat 29g	45%
Saturated 4.0g	20%
Monounsaturated 18g	
Polyunsaturated 4.6g	
Sodium 269mg	11%
Carbohydrate 83g	28%
Fibre 17g	68%
Protein 35g	
Calcium 128mg	12%

Grilled Chicken and Pineapple

Pineapple with a bit of red onion and lime offers a pleasing zest to grilled chicken.

¼ cup (50 mL) juice from canned
   pineapple
2 tsp (10 mL) liquid honey
1 tsp (5 mL) cornstarch
¼ cup (50 mL) chopped red onion
½ tsp (2 mL) grated lime zest
1 tbsp (15 mL) lime juice
2 boneless skinless chicken breasts,
   about 4 oz (125 g) each
2 rings canned pineapple

Measure pineapple juice into a 2-cup (500 mL) glass measure; stir in honey and cornstarch. Microwave on 100% power for 30 to 50 seconds, stirring once, or until thickened and boiling. Stir in onion, lime zest and juice. Let stand while chicken grills.

Grill chicken and pineapple rings over medium coals until chicken is no longer pink in the centre, about 6 minutes on each side. Meanwhile, grill pineapple until lightly browned, about 1 minute on each side. Place chicken and pineapple on serving plates and drizzle with sauce.

Makes 2 servings.

+ Confetti Rice

Rice cooked in chicken broth with savoury vegetables gives added flavour to a basic side dish.

1 ½ tsp (7 mL) canola oil
¼ cup (50 mL) finely chopped carrot
¼ cup (50 mL) finely chopped celery
2 tbsp (25 mL) finely chopped green
   onion
½ cup (125 mL) long-grain rice
1 cup (250 mL) chicken or vegetable
   broth

In a medium saucepan, heat oil over medium heat. Add carrot, celery and onion. Cook for 3 minutes or until vegetables are almost soft. Stir in rice mixing well, then add broth. Bring to a boil; reduce heat, cover and simmer for 15 to 20 minutes or until liquid is absorbed. When done, fluff with fork.

+ Greens with Louis Dressing

Originally created to top a crab salad, this tasty dressing is equally good with romaine lettuce.

2 tbsp (25 mL) mayonnaise
1 tsp (5 mL) milk
1 tsp (5 mL) red wine vinegar
½ tsp (2 mL) tomato paste
Dash of Worcestershire
4 cups (1 L) torn romaine lettuce

In a small bowl, whisk together mayonnaise, milk, vinegar, tomato paste and Worcestershire sauce.

In a salad bowl, place lettuce. Pour dressing over and toss to mix.

+ Kale with Cranberries and Garlic

The bright flavour of cranberries gives a pleasing tartness to the stronger flavour of the kale.

4 cups (1 L) chopped kale leaves
1 tbsp (15 mL) olive oil
2 cloves garlic, minced
2 tbsp (25 mL) dried cranberries

In a large pot of boiling salted water, cook kale for 5 minutes, or until almost tender. Drain in a colander. Add olive oil and garlic to the same pot over medium heat; cook for 30 seconds or until fragrant. Stir in kale and cranberries; cook for 2 minutes or until heated through.

PER SERVING OF MAIN DISH	
Amount	**% Daily Value**
Calories 198	
Fat 2g	3%
Saturated 0.4g	2%
Monounsaturated 0.3g	
Polyunsaturated 0.3g	
Sodium 75mg	3%
Carbohydrate 20g	7%
Fibre 1g	4%
Protein 26g	
Calcium 28mg	3%

PER SERVING WITH SIDE DISHES	
Amount	**% Daily Value**
Calories 661	
Fat 19g	29%
Saturated 2.8g	14%
Monounsaturated 11.9g	
Polyunsaturated 5.2g	
Sodium 654mg	27%
Carbohydrate 88g	29%
Fibre 8g	32%
Protein 39g	
Calcium 288mg	26%

Tofu Sauté with Sweet Peppers, Carrots and Snow Peas

Preparation Time: 10 minutes Cook Time: 15 minutes

Sometimes called the cheese of Asia, tofu is a versatile ingredient that readily takes on other flavours. Firm tofu works best in this colourful dish since the cubes brown nicely without crumbling before the vegetables are added.

1 tbsp (15 mL) canola oil
½ lb (250 g) firm tofu, cut into
    ½-inch (1 cm) cubes
1 small onion, chopped
1 clove garlic, minced
1 carrot, very thinly sliced
1 sweet orange or red pepper,
    chopped
1 tbsp (15 mL) finely grated fresh
    ginger
4 oz (125 g) snow peas
½ cup (125 mL) low-sodium chicken
    broth or water
1 tbsp (15 mL) sodium-reduced soy
    sauce
Pinch red pepper flakes
1 tbsp (15 mL) water
2 tsp (10 mL) cornstarch

In a large nonstick skillet, heat oil over medium-high heat. Add tofu. Cook without stirring for 2 minutes or until nicely browned on one side. Carefully turn cubes to brown on other side, about 2 minutes.

Add onion, garlic, carrot, pepper and ginger. Cook for 3 minutes over medium heat or until slightly soft.

Stir in peas, broth, soy sauce and pepper flakes. Bring to a boil. Cook for 2 minutes or until peas are tender-crisp.

Combine water and cornstarch. Stir into pan. Cook, stirring constantly, for 1 to 2 minutes or until thickened and bubbly. Serve with quinoa, bulgur or rice.

Makes 2 servings.

Terrific Tofu

Tofu is made from soybeans to which is added either a magnesium or calcium salt to form a curd. Magnesium gives a more mellow flavour, but tofu made with calcium is a much better source of this essential nutrient. Tofu is available in several forms. Silken tofu is more fragile than regular tofu and will blend to a smooth purée in a food processor. Regular tofu is labelled soft, firm or extra firm, depending on the amount of liquid that has been pressed from it during processing. You can make tofu more firm by placing the block of tofu on a cutting board over the sink with a second board balanced on top. To hasten the process, add a weight, such as a small can of food, to the top board. Freezing tofu removes even more moisture, making it suitable to crumble over soups or salads.

Amount	% Daily Value
Calories 264	
Fat 13g	20%
Saturated 1.5g	8%
Monounsaturated 5.3g	
Polyunsaturated 5.2g	
Sodium 328mg	14%
Carbohydrate 26g	9%
Fibre 4g	16%
Protein 14g	
Calcium 464mg	42%

+ Quinoa Pilaf with Fennel

Fennel, sometimes sold as anise, gives a pleasing subtle flavour to a quinoa pilaf. Use the remaining half bulb in a stir-fry, or serve it raw on a vegetable platter.

1/2 cup (125 mL) quinoa, rinsed
1/2 tbsp (7 mL) olive oil
1 small shallot, chopped
1/2 fennel bulb, trimmed, cored and
   cut into 1/4 inch (0.5 cm) cubes
1 cup (250 mL) water
2 tbsp (25 mL) dried cranberries

Using a fine sieve, rinse quinoa. Drain and set aside.

  In a small saucepan, heat oil over medium heat. Add shallot and fennel and cook, stirring occasionally, for 5 minutes or until fennel is slightly soft. Add quinoa and water, bring to a boil, reduce heat, cover and simmer for 12 minutes or until liquid is almost absorbed. Remove from heat, stir in cranberries and let stand about 10 minutes.

+ Mediterranean Tomato Slices

When field-ripened tomatoes are available, this simple dressing is all that is needed for a memorable side dish.

2 ripe tomatoes, sliced
1 tsp (5 mL) balsamic vinegar
1 tsp (5 mL) olive oil
Chopped fresh oregano, basil, thyme
  or tarragon

Drizzle tomatoes with vinegar and olive oil. Sprinkle with fresh herbs.

PER SERVING WITH SIDE DISHES	
Amount	% Daily Value
Calories 537	
Fat 22g	34%
Saturated 2.5g	13%
Monounsaturated 10.2g	
Polyunsaturated 6.8g	
Sodium 380mg	16%
Carbohydrate 71g	24%
Fibre 11g	44%
Protein 22g	
Calcium 529mg	48%

Chicken with Wine and Sweet Potatoes

Preparation Time: 10 minutes Cook Time: 35 minutes

The ingredients in this economical dish combine to make a fine-flavoured meal that is elegant enough for a special occasion. If you don't have sweet potatoes, replace them with thickly sliced carrots.

2 chicken legs, about 5 oz (140 g) each
1 tsp (5 mL) canola oil
2 shallots, peeled
1 sweet potato, peeled and cut in thick slices
1/2 cup (125 mL) dry white wine or apple juice
6 to 8 pitted prunes
1 tsp (5 mL) finely grated fresh ginger
1/4 tsp (1 mL) ground cumin
1/8 tsp (0.5 mL) salt
Pinch ground black pepper
Chopped fresh parsley for garnish

Remove skin and fat from chicken and discard.

In a medium nonstick skillet, heat oil over medium heat; brown chicken on all sides. Add shallots; cook for 1 to 2 minutes.

Add sweet potato, wine, prunes, ginger, cumin, salt and pepper. Cover and bring to a boil; reduce heat and simmer for 25 to 30 minutes or until chicken is cooked and sweet potato is tender. Sprinkle with parsley and serve.

Makes 2 servings.

+ Peas with Garlic and Thyme

Fresh thyme and a touch of garlic enliven tender sweet peas.

1 tsp (5 mL) olive oil
1 clove garlic, chopped
1 1/2 cups (375 mL) frozen small peas
1 tbsp (15 mL) chopped fresh thyme or 1 tsp (5 mL) dried
1 tbsp (15 mL) water

In a small skillet, heat olive oil over medium-low heat. Add garlic and cook for 2 minutes or until golden. Stir in peas, thyme and water. Bring to a boil; reduce heat and boil gently for 3 minutes or until liquid is evaporated and peas are tender.

Vitamin A Ups and Downs

For most of us, our daily intake of vitamin A fluctuates considerably. Because vitamin A is fat soluble and can be stored, the daily intake is less critical than water-soluble vitamins like vitamin C. While animal products provide us with the active form of vitamin A, our bodies make most of the vitamin A we need from orange and green plant foods that are rich in carotenoids, especially beta-carotene. Although eating a balanced diet with at least five servings of vegetables and fruit will provide enough vitamin A, we rely to a large extent on a few star sources. Sweet potatoes are one of them. In this meal they provide more than the daily requirement of vitamin A.

+ Cabbage Salad with Buttermilk Dressing

Buttermilk makes a pleasing tangy dressing for a simple cabbage salad. Replace buttermilk with plain yogurt if desired.

¹/₄ cup (50 mL) buttermilk
1 tbsp (15 mL) light mayonnaise
1 tbsp (15 mL) cider vinegar
1 ¹/₂ tsp (7 mL) granulated sugar
2 cups (500 mL) thinly sliced cabbage
1 tbsp (15 mL) minced sweet onion or
   shallot
3 radishes, thinly sliced
1 celery stalk, sliced

In a medium bowl, whisk together buttermilk, mayonnaise, vinegar and sugar. Add cabbage, onion, radishes and celery. Toss to mix.

PER SERVING OF MAIN DISH	
Amount	% Daily Value
Calories 359	
Fat 8g	12%
Saturated 1.5g	8%
Monounsaturated 3.0g	
Polyunsaturated 2.1g	
Sodium 305mg	13%
Carbohydrate 36g	12%
Fibre 5g	20%
Protein 28g	
Calcium 62mg	6%

PER SERVING WITH SIDE DISHES	
Amount	% Daily Value
Calories 585	
Fat 12g	18%
Saturated 2.3g	12%
Monounsaturated 4.8g	
Polyunsaturated 2.7g	
Sodium 537mg	22%
Carbohydrate 76g	25%
Fibre 15g	60%
Protein 39g	
Calcium 259mg	24%

Grilled Spice-Rubbed Pork Chops

Preparation Time: 5 minutes Cook Time: 10 minutes

This rub of fragrant spices is an easy way to enhance the flavour of grilled pork without being overpowering.

1 tbsp (15 mL) ground cumin
1 tbsp (15 mL) ground coriander
2 tsp (10 mL) olive oil
2 cloves garlic, minced
2 centre-cut pork chops with bone,
  about 5 oz (150 g) each, or 1
  butterfly chop, about 8 oz (250 g)
  cut in half

In a small bowl, combine cumin, coriander, oil and garlic. Rub over surface of pork chops.

Grill chops over medium-high heat for 5 minutes per side, or until inside is no longer pink.

Makes 2 servings.

Trim the Fat

! To reduce the amount of saturated fat, trim away as much of the visible fat as possible from pork, beef and lamb.

+ Brown Rice Pilaf

A simple pilaf with the goodness of whole grain.

1 ½ cups (300 mL) water
½ cup (125 mL) brown rice
2 tsp (10 mL) canola oil
3 to 4 mushrooms, chopped
½ small onion, chopped
1 clove garlic, minced
1 sprig parsley, chopped

In a small saucepan, bring water to a boil. Add brown rice, reduce heat, cover and simmer for 40 minutes or until tender. Meanwhile, in a small skillet, heat oil over medium heat. Add mushrooms, onion and garlic. Cook for 5 minutes or until vegetables are tender; stir in parsley and rice.

+ Green Beans and Cauliflower with Red Onion

Red, green and white combine for a colourful vegetable medley.

1 cup (250 mL) whole green beans
1 cup (250 mL) cauliflower florets
1 tsp (5 mL) canola oil
⅓ cup (75 mL) chopped red onion
1 tbsp (15 mL) finely chopped
  fresh parsley
Salt and ground black pepper

Steam beans and cauliflower for 5 to 7 minutes or until tender but firm. Drain and transfer to serving dish. Meanwhile, in a small microwave-safe dish, combine oil and red onion. Microwave on 100% power for 1 minute or just until tender. Stir in parsley. Season with salt and pepper to taste.

+ Spinach Salad with Orange Ginger Dressing

A spirited ginger dressing for a delicious and nutritious salad.

2 tbsp (25 mL) frozen orange juice
   concentrate

2 tbsp (25 mL) water

1 tbsp (15 mL) rice wine vinegar

1 tsp (5 mL) finely grated fresh ginger

1 tsp (5 mL) sesame oil

½ tsp (2 mL) soy sauce

½ tsp (2 mL) honey

4 cups (1 L) torn fresh spinach

1 carrot, grated

In a small bowl, whisk together orange juice concentrate, water, vinegar, ginger, sesame oil, soy sauce and honey. Set aside.

In a salad bowl, combine spinach and carrot. Toss with dressing.

PER SERVING OF MAIN DISH		PER SERVING WITH SIDE DISHES	
Amount	% Daily Value	Amount	% Daily Value
Calories 224		Calories 609	
Fat 12g	18%	Fat 24g	37%
Saturated 3.1g	16%	Saturated 4.3g	22%
Monounsaturated 6.6g		Monounsaturated 12.1g	
Polyunsaturated 1.2g		Polyunsaturated 5.0g	
Sodium 73mg	3%	Sodium 262mg	11%
Carbohydrate 3g	1%	Carbohydrate 68g	23%
Fibre 0g	0%	Fibre 9g	36%
Protein 25g		Protein 35g	
Calcium 64mg	6%	Calcium 215mg	20%

Indonesian-Style Chicken with Savoury Peanut Sauce

Preparation Time: 10 minutes Cook Time: 25 minutes

Coated with a savoury peanut sauce, chicken breasts take on the popular flavour of Indonesian satay.

2 tbsp (25 mL) smooth peanut butter
1 tbsp (15 mL) tomato paste
2 tsp (10 mL) lightly packed brown sugar
2 tsp (10 mL) lemon juice
1 1/2 tsp (7 mL) chopped fresh oregano or 1/2 tsp (2 mL) dried
1/2 tsp (2 mL) ground cinnamon
1 small clove garlic, minced
2 tbsp (25 mL) water
1 tsp (5 mL) canola oil
2 skinless boneless chicken breasts, about 4 oz (125 g) each
1 tbsp (15 mL) chopped unsalted peanuts
2 green onions, sliced

Preheat oven to 400°F (200°C). In a small microwave-safe container, combine peanut butter, tomato paste, brown sugar, lemon juice, oregano, cinnamon, garlic and water. Microwave on 100% power, stirring frequently, for 30 seconds or until boiling. Whisk to blend.

In a small ovenproof skillet, heat oil over medium-high heat. Add chicken and brown for 2 minutes per side or until golden. Spread sauce over chicken and bake for 20 to 30 minutes or until chicken is no longer pink inside. Transfer to a serving plate and sprinkle with peanuts and green onions.

Makes 2 servings.

Clean and Separate for Food Safety

Raw poultry as well as all raw meats and seafood contain naturally occurring bacteria. When cutting these foods, be sure to wash the cutting board and knives in very hot soapy water to avoid spreading these bacteria. Keep raw poultry, meat and seafood well away from other foods, especially any that will be served uncooked. When it is properly cooked, chicken pieces have no traces of pink and reach an internal temperature of 165°F (74°C).

+ Basmati Rice with Chutney

Rice with a flavourful chutney nicely complements the peanut chicken.

1 cup (250 mL) water
1/8 tsp (0.5 mL) salt
1/2 cup (125 mL) basmati rice
2 tbsp (25 mL) chutney

In a medium saucepan, place water and salt. Bring to a boil and stir in rice. Return to a boil; reduce heat, cover and simmer for 15 to 20 minutes or until rice is soft and the liquid is absorbed. Stir in chutney.

+ Steamed Green Beans

A splash of olive oil enhances fresh green beans. If fresh aren't available, frozen cut green beans are a good alternative.

1 ½ cups (375 mL) whole green beans
¼ cup (50 mL) water
1 tsp (5 mL) olive oil
Ground black pepper

In a small saucepan, bring beans and water to a boil; reduce heat, cover and boil gently for 7 minutes or until tender but firm. Drain and drizzle with olive oil and a sprinkle of freshly ground black pepper.

+ Kohlrabi and Carrot Salad with Orange and Cumin

Raw kohlrabi is an amiable partner in a salad with grated carrots enhanced by orange and the tang of cumin. Sunflower seeds add extra crunch and nutrition.

¼ cup (50 mL) orange juice
1 tbsp (15 mL) fresh lemon juice
1 tbsp (15 mL) olive oil
½ tsp (2 mL) ground cumin
¼ tsp (1 mL) granulated sugar
Salt and ground black pepper
1 cup (250 mL) grated kohlrabi
1 cup (250 mL) grated carrot
1 tbsp (15 mL) roasted shelled
   sunflower seeds

In a salad bowl, whisk together orange juice, lemon juice, olive oil, cumin, sugar and salt and pepper to taste. Stir in kohlrabi, carrot and sunflower seeds.

PER SERVING OF MAIN DISH	
Amount	% Daily Value
Calories 301	
Fat 15g	23%
Saturated 2.6g	13%
Monounsaturated 7.0g	
Polyunsaturated 4.2g	
Sodium 74mg	3%
Carbohydrate 13g	4%
Fibre 2g	8%
Protein 31g	
Calcium 54mg	5%

PER SERVING WITH SIDE DISHES	
Amount	% Daily Value
Calories 684	
Fat 27g	42%
Saturated 4.2g	21%
Monounsaturated 14.2g	
Polyunsaturated 6.5g	
Sodium 280mg	12%
Carbohydrate 77g	26%
Fibre 10g	40%
Protein 39g	
Calcium 146mg	13%

Southwest Taco Beef over Rice

Preparation Time: 10 minutes Cook Time: 15 minutes

A fast and satisfying main dish that will soon become a favourite if you enjoy Mexican flavours. Salsa can bring high levels of sodium, so check the nutrient labels and choose a brand with an acceptable level, or make your own. The analysis for this recipe is based on a salsa with 75 mg of sodium in 2 tablespoons (30 mL).

6 oz (170 g) lean ground beef
1 small onion, chopped
¾ cups (175 mL) mild or hot salsa
⅓ cup (75 mL) water
2 tbsp (25 mL) tomato paste
½ tsp (2 mL) ground cumin
Salt and ground black pepper
2 cups (500 mL) hot cooked rice
1 tomato, chopped
2 tbsp (25 mL) shredded Cheddar
   cheese
16 tortilla chips (optional)

In a medium nonstick skillet over medium-high heat, brown beef and onion until beef is no longer pink.

Add salsa, water, tomato paste and cumin. Bring to a boil; reduce heat, cover and simmer for 5 minutes. Add salt and pepper to taste.

Mound rice on 2 serving plates and top with beef mixture. Top with chopped tomato and shredded cheese; arrange tortilla chips on side if desired.

Makes 2 servings.

+ Grapefruit Salad with Currant Glaze

Currant jelly makes a colourful and tasty topping for a grapefruit salad. The addition of a few pomegranate seeds adds special interest.

1 tbsp (15 mL) currant jelly
½ tsp (2 mL) lemon juice
2 to 3 romaine lettuce leaves
1 large pink grapefruit
Pomegranate seeds (optional)

In a small bowl, whisk together currant jelly and lemon juice. Set aside.

Line two salad plates with lettuce leaves. Remove outside rind from grapefruit with a sharp knife, exposing the pulp. Carefully cut on both sides of each inner membrane and lift out the fruit sections. Arrange sections on each plate and drizzle with dressing. Garnish with a few pomegranate seeds if desired.

PER SERVING OF MAIN DISHES			PER SERVING WITH SIDE DISHES		
Amount	% Daily Value		Amount	% Daily Value	
Calories 510			Calories 593		
Fat 15g	23%		Fat 15g	23%	
Saturated 6.3g	32%		Saturated 6.3g	32%	
Monounsaturated 6.4g			Monounsaturated 6.4g		
Polyunsaturated 0.9g			Polyunsaturated 0.9g		
Sodium 347mg	14%		Sodium 352mg	15%	
Carbohydrate 62g	21%		Carbohydrate 83g	28%	
Fibre 3g	12%		Fibre 5g	20%	
Protein 25g			Protein 26g		
Calcium 103mg	9%		Calcium 137mg	12%	

Go Red

Red and white grapefruit are equal on the vitamin C and calorie fronts, but red has 25 per cent more beta carotene as well as some lycopene.

QUICK WAYS WITH FILLETS

Preparation Time: 5 to 10 minutes Cook Time: 5 to 10 minutes

Fish fillets cook in just minutes in a microwave, making a great meal for two. These small recipes make it easy to have fish more often. We like them served with cooked brown rice, whole grain couscous or quinoa. Allow one cup of cooked grain per person.

Use fresh or individually frozen fillets of sole, cod, halibut, mahi mahi, tilapia, blue fish or red snapper to prepare any of the following for two servings.

Fillets Asian-Style

2 tsp (10 mL) sodium-reduced
  soy sauce
1 tsp (5 mL) sesame oil
1/2 tsp (2 mL) finely chopped fresh
  ginger (optional)
8 oz (250 g) fish fillets
4 green onions, sliced

In a small flat microwave-safe dish, combine soy sauce, sesame oil and ginger if using. Add fillets, turning to coat with sauce, and top with green onions. Cover with plastic wrap. Microwave on 100% power for 2 to 3 minutes or until fish flakes easily with a fork.

Fillets Parmesan

2 tbsp (25 mL) Panko or other dry
  bread crumbs
1 tbsp (15 mL) grated Parmesan
  cheese
1/2 tsp (2 mL) each: dried oregano and
  dried basil
8 oz (250 g) fish fillets

On a flat plate or piece of wax paper, combine Panko, cheese, oregano, and basil. Coat fillets with crumbs and transfer to a small flat microwave-safe dish. Cover with a paper towel. Microwave on 100% power for 2 to 3 minutes or until fish flakes easily with a fork.

Fillets Almondine

2 tbsp (25 mL) slivered almonds,
  divided
1 tbsp (15 mL) butter
8 oz (250 g) fish fillets

In a small microwave-safe dish, combine almonds and butter. Microwave on 100% power, stirring once, for 40 seconds to 1 minute or until almonds are golden brown. Place fish in a small flat microwave-safe dish. Drain butter from almonds and pour over fish. Cover with plastic wrap. Microwave on 100% power for 2 to 3 minutes or until fish flakes easily with a fork. Sprinkle almonds over fillets before serving.

Go Fish

While fish have been on our dinner plates for generations, recently more species have become popular. Mahi mahi is a relative newcomer. Although the common name is "dolphin-fish," mahi mahi is a fish and is not at all related to the dolphin family of mammals. To avoid any confusion, the Hawaiian name "mahi mahi" has come to be generally accepted. Mahi mahi has firm, flavourful flesh and is a sustainable choice as they are fast growing, live short lives and can withstand high fishing pressure.

QUICK FILLETS PARMESAN

PER SERVING WITH
1 CUP (250 mL) COOKED
BROWN RICE

Amount	% Daily Value
Calories 346	
Fat 4g	6%
Saturated 1.2g	6%
Monounsaturated 1.1g	
Polyunsaturated 1.0g	
Sodium 162mg	7%
Carbohydrate 47g	16%
Fibre 3g	12%
Protein 28g	
Calcium 78mg	7%

QUICK FILLETS ALMONDINE

PER SERVING WITH
1 CUP (250 mL) COOKED
BROWN RICE

Amount	% Daily Value
Calories 409	
Fat 12g	18%
Saturated 4.6g	23%
Monounsaturated 4.8g	
Polyunsaturated 2.0g	
Sodium 162mg	7%
Carbohydrate 46g	15%
Fibre 4g	16%
Protein 28g	
Calcium 56mg	5%

QUICK FILLETS ASIAN-STYLE

PER SERVING WITH
1 CUP (250 mL) COOKED
BROWN RICE

Amount	% Daily Value
Calories 350	
Fat 5g	8%
Saturated 1.0g	5%
Monounsaturated 1.8g	
Polyunsaturated 2.0g	
Sodium 284mg	12%
Carbohydrate 47g	16%
Fibre 4g	16%
Protein 27g	
Calcium 62mg	6%

Argentine-Style Burgers with Chimichurri Sauce

Preparation Time: 10 minutes Cook Time: 15 minutes

In many Latin American countries, grilled meat is often served with chimichurri, a zesty pesto-like sauce that originated in Argentina. Made from fresh parsley, it is a source of essential nutrients and has a memorable flavour. Adding crushed corn chips instead of the usual bread crumbs gives these burgers an appealing crunch and an intriguing Latin flavour.

Burgers:

1 egg white
1/4 cup (50 mL) crushed baked corn chips
2 tbsp (25 mL) mild or hot salsa
1 clove garlic, minced
2 green onions, finely chopped
1 tsp (5 mL) chopped fresh oregano or 1/4 tsp (1 mL) dried
1 tsp (5 mL) chopped fresh thyme or 1/4 tsp (1 mL) dried
1/2 tsp (2 mL) paprika
8 oz (250 g) ground turkey or beef
2 burger buns, toasted

Sauce:

1/2 cup (125 mL) finely chopped fresh parsley
1 small clove garlic, finely chopped
2 tsp (10 mL) olive oil
1/2 tsp (2 mL) red wine vinegar
Salt and ground black pepper

Burgers:

Preheat grill to medium. In a medium bowl, lightly beat egg white. Mix in chips, salsa, garlic, onions, oregano, thyme and paprika. Add turkey and mix well.

Form into 2 patties about 3/4 inch (2 cm) thick. Grill for 6 minutes per side, or until a rapid-read thermometer inserted sideways into the centre of each patty reads 160°F (71°C).

Sauce:

In a small bowl, mix parsley and garlic. Stir in oil and vinegar; add salt and pepper to taste.

Spread each patty with chimichurri sauce and serve on buns.

Makes 2 servings

PER SERVING OF MAIN DISH	
Amount	% Daily Value
Calories 369	
Fat 17g	26%
Saturated 3.8g	19%
Monounsaturated 7.5g	
Polyunsaturated 4.3g	
Sodium 466mg	19%
Carbohydrate 27g	9%
Fibre 2g	8%
Protein 27g	
Calcium 118mg	11%

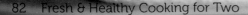

+ Baked Squash Rings with Ginger-Honey Glaze 🎥

Ginger and honey add an exciting dimension to rings of baked squash.

1 small acorn squash
2 tbsp (25 mL) honey
2 tsp (10 mL) sodium-reduced soy
  sauce
1 tsp (5 mL) rice vinegar
1 tsp (5 mL) finely grated fresh ginger
1 small clove garlic, minced

Preheat oven to 450°F (230°C). Cut squash into four rings; remove and discard seeds. Line a baking sheet with foil and spray with canola oil; arrange rings on foil. Cover squash with a second sheet of foil and bake for 15 minutes or until squash begins to soften.

In a small bowl, combine honey, soy sauce, vinegar, ginger and garlic. Brush mixture over squash and return, uncovered, to oven. Bake for 5 minutes and brush again with honey mixture. Bake for 3 to 5 minutes longer or until squash is brown, tender and glazed.

> ## Ginger Storage
> ⓘ Freeze pieces of fresh ginger, sometimes called gingerroot, in a small covered container. Then defrost slightly and grate as needed.

PER SERVING WITH SIDE DISHES	
Amount	**% Daily Value**
Calories 527	
Fat 17g	26%
Saturated 3.8g	19%
Monounsaturated 7.5g	
Polyunsaturated 4.4g	
Sodium 652mg	27%
Carbohydrate 68g	23%
Fibre 6g	24%
Protein 29g	
Calcium 194mg	18%

Wine-Braised Lamb Shoulder Chops

Preparation Time: 10 minutes Cook Time: 55 minutes

Inexpensive shoulder lamb chops have great flavour and become very tender when braised. Red wine and herbs de Provence make a savoury dish that is nicely complemented by onion-studded mashed potatoes.

2 lamb shoulder chops, about 6 oz
  (170 g) each
Salt and ground black pepper
1 tsp (5 mL) olive oil
2 cloves garlic, chopped
1 sweet green pepper, sliced
1/2 cup (125 mL) dry red wine
1 tbsp (15 mL) tomato paste
1 tsp (5 mL) chopped fresh thyme or
  1/4 tsp (1 mL) dried
1 tsp (5 mL) chopped fresh basil or
  1/4 tsp (1 mL) dried
1/2 tsp (2 mL) chopped fresh rosemary
  or 1/8 tsp (0.5 mL) dried

Sprinkle chops with salt and pepper if desired. In a medium skillet, heat oil over medium-high heat. Add chops and brown about 2 minutes on each side. Remove chops from pan and set aside.

Reduce heat to medium and add garlic and green pepper; cook until soft but not browned, about 1 minute. Stir in wine, tomato paste, thyme, basil and rosemary. Add chops and bring to a boil; reduce heat, cover and simmer for 45 minutes or until chops are tender. Remove chops to warm plates and return pan to heat. Boil gently for several minutes to slightly reduce the sauce. Serve chops with sauce and green peppers.

Makes 2 servings.

+ Onion-Studded Mashed Potatoes

Green onions add a subtle flavour to mashed potatoes. Leave the skins on the potatoes for good texture and more fibre.

2 to 3 unpeeled red potatoes,
  quartered
3 green onions, sliced
2 to 3 tbsp (25 to 45 mL) plain yogurt
Salt and ground black pepper

In a medium pot of boiling water, cook potatoes and green onions for 15 minutes or until potatoes are tender. Drain and stir in yogurt; mash until smooth. Add salt and pepper to taste.

PER SERVING OF MAIN DISH	
Amount	% Daily Value
Calories 285	
Fat 12g	18%
Saturated 3.9g	20%
Monounsaturated 5.6g	
Polyunsaturated 1.2g	
Sodium 104mg	4%
Carbohydrate 7g	2%
Fibre 2g	8%
Protein 26g	
Calcium 44mg	4%

PER SERVING WITH SIDE DISHES	
Amount	% Daily Value
Calories 729	
Fat 28g	43%
Saturated 6.6g	33%
Monounsaturated 16.1g	
Polyunsaturated 2.8g	
Sodium 353mg	15%
Carbohydrate 76g	25%
Fibre 13g	52%
Protein 40g	
Calcium 214mg	19%

+ Sliced Brussels Sprouts with Parmesan

Sautéed in a bit of olive oil and topped with a sprinkling of Parmesan, these tiny cabbages make a tasty and nutritious side dish. Slicing them before cooking ensures quick, even cooking.

2 cups (500 mL) fresh Brussels
  sprouts (or defrosted frozen sprouts)
1 to 2 tbsp (15 to 25 mL) olive oil
1/4 cup (50 mL) chopped red onion
1 tbsp (15 mL) grated Parmesan
  cheese

Cut Brussels sprouts into approximately 1/8 inch (3 mm) slices. In a small skillet, heat olive oil over medium heat. Add red onion and cook for 1 minute or until almost soft. Stir in the Brussels sprouts; stir-fry for 8 to 10 minutes or until tender. Sprinkle with cheese before serving.

Bulgur Salad with Mint

A simple tabbouleh salad to make when mint first appears in your garden. If you have a ripe tomato, add it for a splash of colour and flavour.

1/2 cup (125 mL) bulgur
1/8 tsp (1/2 mL) salt
3/4 cup (175 mL) boiling water
1 1/2 tbsp (22 mL) fresh lemon juice
1 tbsp (15 mL) olive oil
2 tbsp (25 mL) chopped fresh mint
2 tbsp (25 mL) chopped fresh parsley
2 green onions, minced
Salt and ground black pepper

In a medium bowl, combine bulgur and salt. Pour boiling water over and let stand for 12 minutes.

In a small bowl, whisk together lemon juice and olive oil. Pour over bulgur, mixing well. Stir in mint, parsley and green onions. Add salt and pepper to taste.

STIR-FRY QUARTET

Preparation Time: 10 minutes Cook Time: 15 minutes

Stir-frys are quick, versatile and make a perfect meal for two. In just a few minutes, you can turn a small amount of meat, whatever veggies you have in the fridge and a few condiments into a satisfying, flavourful and healthy meal. Round out the meal with a simple cucumber salad (page 90).

Beef and Asparagus Stir-Fry

When asparagus is featured in your market, indulge in this classic dish that takes just minutes to prepare.

8 oz (250 g) top sirloin, sliced into thin strips
1 tsp (5 mL) cornstarch
1 tbsp (15 mL) canola oil, divided
1 tsp (5 mL) sesame oil
8 oz (250 g) thin asparagus, trimmed and cut into 1 ½ inch (3 cm) pieces, about 2 cups (500 mL)
2 cloves garlic, minced
¼ cup (50 mL) sliced red or green onions
2 tbsp (25 mL) finely grated fresh ginger
¼ cup (50 mL) water
1 tbsp (15 mL) sodium-reduced soy sauce
2 cups (500 mL) hot cooked rice or quinoa

In a medium bowl, combine beef and cornstarch, mixing to coat evenly.

In a nonstick skillet, heat half of canola oil over medium-high heat. Add beef; cook without stirring for 1 minute or until brown on one side. Turn and cook second side for 1 minute or until brown. Transfer to a plate.

Add sesame oil and remaining canola oil to skillet; heat over medium-high heat. Add asparagus, garlic, onion, ginger; cook for 2 minutes or until vegetables are tender-crisp. Stir in water and soy sauce; heat to boiling and add beef. Serve over hot rice or quinoa.

Makes 2 servings.

Chill Out

To cut beef into thin slices more easily, first place in the freezer for 20 to 30 minutes.

Keep it Lean

A good practice when cooking beef is to remove as much of the visible fat as possible. Contrary to popular belief, the type of animal fat varies and it is not all saturated. Over half the total fat in beef is in the form of monounsaturated and polyunsaturated fatty acids. For pork, about 60 per cent of the fat is unsaturated while that in chicken rates about 68 per cent. The range in fish is from 70 to 80 per cent. However, whether saturated or unsaturated, the calorie count of fatty acids is the same. So keep it lean.

PER SERVING OF MAIN DISH	
Amount	% Daily Value
Calories 474	
Fat 14g	22%
Saturated 2.5g	13%
Monounsaturated 6.8g	
Polyunsaturated 3.4g	
Sodium 343mg	14%
Carbohydrate 54g	18%
Fibre 4g	16%
Protein 32g	
Calcium 74mg	7%

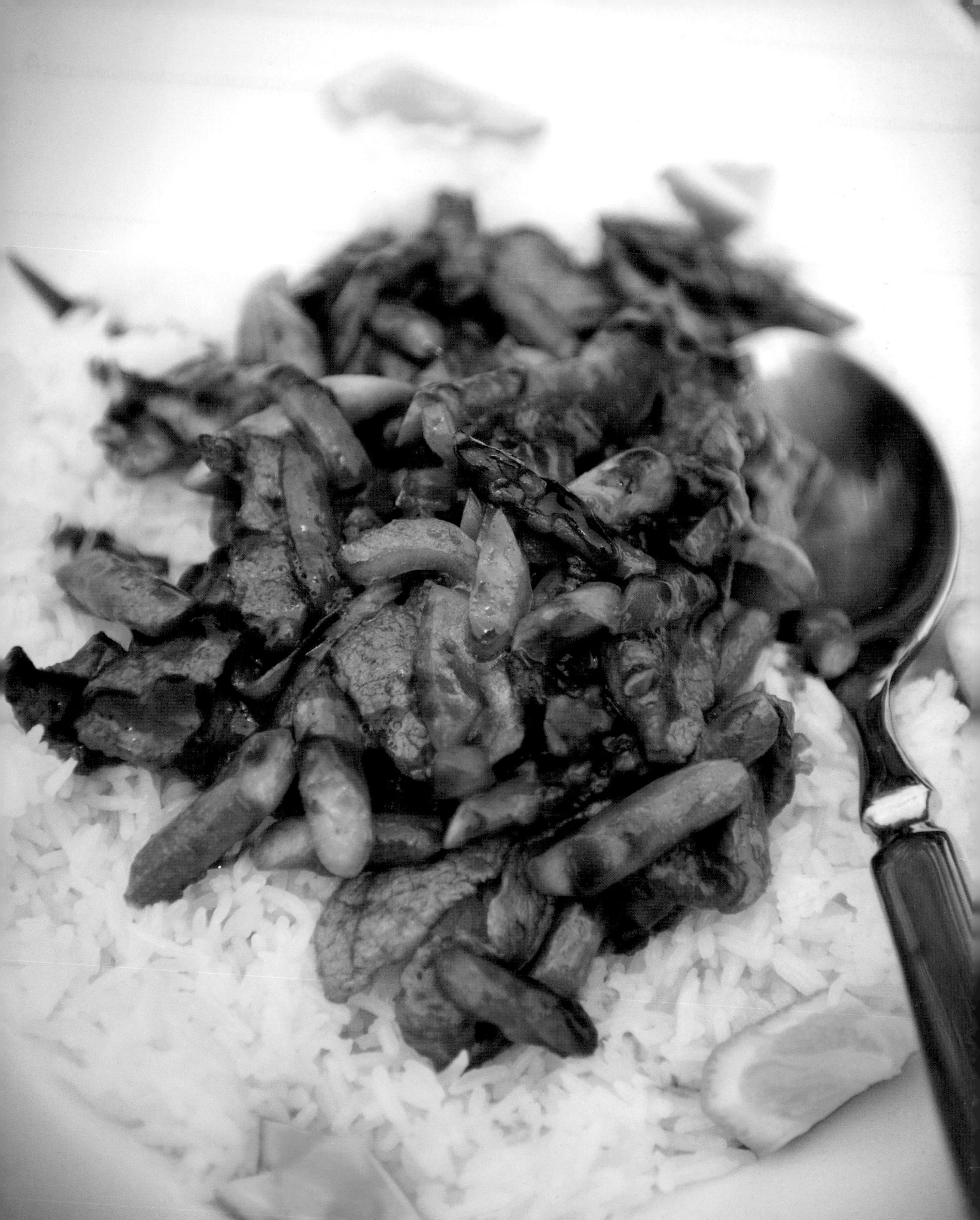

Chicken Bok Choy Stir-Fry

The mild flavour of bok choy is delicious for a quick stir-fry with chicken. To kick up the flavour, we used red chili paste, a product of Thailand that is not as fiery as its name would suggest. Or use any hot pepper garlic sauce, but watch the sodium — and the heat!

1 tbsp (15 mL) canola oil

8 oz (250 g) boneless chicken breast, cut into thin strips

1 small onion, sliced

2 cloves garlic, minced

12 oz (375 g) bok choy, sliced, about 4 cups (1 L)

½ cup (125 mL) water or chicken broth

1 ½ tsp (7 mL) hot chili paste

1 tsp (5 mL) sodium-reduced soy sauce

1 tbsp (15 mL) cornstarch

1 tbsp (15 mL) water

2 cups (500 mL) hot cooked rice or quinoa

In a large nonstick skillet, heat oil over medium-high heat. Add chicken; cook, turning several times, for 3 minutes or until no longer pink.

Add onion and garlic; cook for 2 minutes or until soft. Stir in bok choy, water, hot chili paste and soy sauce. Bring to a boil; reduce heat, cover, and cook for 3 minutes or until vegetables are tender-crisp.

In a small bowl, combine cornstarch and water. Stir into vegetables; bring to a boil, stirring constantly. Serve over hot rice or quinoa.

Makes 2 servings.

PER SERVING OF MAIN DISH	
Amount	% Daily Value
Calories 468	
Fat 10g	15%
Saturated 1.2g	6%
Monounsaturated 4.8g	
Polyunsaturated 2.8g	
Sodium 314mg	13%
Carbohydrate 60g	20%
Fibre 3g	12%
Protein 33g	
Calcium 222mg	20%

Bok Choy

Bok choy is one of the best-known Chinese vegetables. It has a very mild flavour and the snow-white stems and dark green leaves are packed with powerful antioxidants as well as healthy amounts of folate, and vitamins C and A. Baby bok choy is a smaller version of regular bok choy. Its sweet buttery flavour is delicious in stir-frys with beef, chicken or shrimp.

Orange Beef Stir-Fry

Mandarin oranges add bright colour and refreshing taste to a quick beef stir-fry.

8 oz (250 g) sirloin or top round steak

1/2 cup (125 mL) orange juice

1 1/2 tbsp (22 mL) sodium-reduced soy sauce

2 tsp (10 mL) finely grated fresh ginger or 1/4 tsp (1 mL) ground ginger

1 tbsp (15 mL) canola oil

1 small onion, thinly sliced

1 clove garlic, minced

6 oz (170 g) green beans, cut in 1-inch (2.5 cm) lengths

1/3 cup (75 mL) low-sodium beef broth or water

1 tbsp (15 mL) cornstarch

2 green onions, cut in 1-inch (2.5 cm) pieces

1 can (10 oz/284 mL) mandarin oranges, drained

2 cups (500 mL) hot cooked rice or quinoa

Cut beef into thin slices across the grain.

In a medium bowl, combine orange juice, soy sauce and ginger. Add beef; let stand for 30 minutes.

In a nonstick skillet or wok, heat oil over high heat. Drain beef, reserving marinade. Stir-fry beef, onion and garlic for 2 minutes or until beef is no longer pink. Remove beef mixture from skillet and set aside.

Add beans and broth to skillet. Bring to a boil; reduce heat, cover and boil gently for 3 minutes.

Combine cornstarch with remaining marinade and stir into skillet. Add green onions and bring to a boil, stirring constantly. Gently fold in reserved beef and oranges; return to a boil. Serve over hot rice or quinoa.

Makes 2 servings.

PER SERVING OF MAIN DISH	
Amount	**% Daily Value**
Calories 570	
Fat 12g	18%
Saturated 2.3g	12%
Monounsaturated 5.9g	
Polyunsaturated 2.5g	
Sodium 506mg	21%
Carbohydrate 82g	27%
Fibre 6g	24%
Protein 33g	
Calcium 129mg	12%

Zinc, Part of the Beef Bonus

Meat is a prime source of zinc. Zinc is also found in plant foods, but is poorly absorbed, so shying away from meat may leave you short of this mineral. This is often a problem for young women, vegetarians and the not-so-young who may need extra zinc to fulfill their dietary needs. Best known for wound healing and healthy immune functioning, zinc is a key component of about 100 enzymes, so include a good food source in your meal plan.

Soy Sauce Savvy

This recipe derives much of its flavour from soy sauce. But to keep sodium under control, we used a sodium-reduced version. A tablespoon of regular soy sauce has 835 to 1010 mg of sodium compared to 535 mg for sodium-reduced (or light) soy sauce.

Shrimp and Rapini Stir-Fry

Rapini is a long, thin-stemmed relative of broccoli. With its mild taste, it is delicious in a stir-fry. But if it isn't available, broccoli florets or asparagus will shine just as well.

1 tbsp (15 mL) canola oil, divided

8 oz (250 g) fresh or uncooked frozen shelled shrimp, about 10 oz (280 g) with shells

2 tsp (10 mL) finely grated fresh ginger

1 tsp (5 mL) minced garlic

1/4 cup (50 mL) water

2 tbsp (25 mL) hoisin sauce

1 tsp (5 mL) sodium-reduced soy sauce

1/4 tsp (1 mL) hot pepper sauce or dried red pepper flakes

8 oz (250 g) rapini, cut into 1/2-inch (1 cm) thick slices, about 3 cups (750 mL)

2 cups (500 mL) hot cooked rice or quinoa

In a large nonstick skillet, heat half the oil over medium-high heat. Add shrimp and cook for 3 minutes or until pink, stirring frequently. Transfer to a plate.

Add remaining oil to skillet; add ginger and garlic, stirring, for 1 minute. Add water, hoisin sauce, soy sauce and hot pepper sauce; bring to a boil, stirring to mix. Stir in rapini, cover and cook for 2 minutes or just until tender. Stir in shrimp and cook until heated through. Serve over hot rice or quinoa.

Makes 2 servings.

Cucumbers and Yogurt Topping

An easy version of raita, the popular Indian salad. Add spices such as black mustard or cumin seeds for different flavours.

1/2 seedless cucumber, sliced

1/4 cup (50 mL) plain yogurt

Splash of tarragon or other flavoured vinegar

Salt

Sugar

Place cucumber on a serving dish. In a small bowl, combine yogurt with vinegar and a pinch of salt and sugar. Pour over cucumber slices.

SHRIMP & RAPINI STIR-FRY PER SERVING		
Amount		% Daily Value
Calories 448		
Fat 10g		15%
Saturated 1.1g		6%
Monounsaturated 4.6g		
Polyunsaturated 3.2g		
Sodium 556mg		23%
Carbohydrate 56g		19%
Fibre 4g		116%
Protein 31g		
Calcium 203mg		18%

CUCUMBER AND YOGURT TOPPING PER SERVING		
Amount		% Daily Value
Calories 54		
Fat 1g		2%
Saturated 0.4g		2%
Monounsaturated 0.1g		
Polyunsaturated 0.1g		
Sodium 26mg		1%
Carbohydrate 11g		4%
Fibre 2g		8%
Protein 3g		
Calcium 92mg		8%

Shrimp Fettuccine with Fresh Basil Pesto and Zucchini

Preparation Time: 5 minutes Cook Time: 15 minutes

A colourful and delicious dish that is quick to make. Pasta, shrimp and vegetables enhanced by a savoury pesto cook together in one pot.

6 oz (170 g) fettuccine or spaghetti

8 oz (250 g) uncooked frozen shelled shrimp, about 10 oz (280 g) with shells

1 small zucchini, cut into matchsticks

1/2 red pepper, cut in strips

3 tbsp (45 mL) basil pesto (recipe below)

2 tbsp (25 mL) grated Parmesan cheese

1/2 tsp (2 mL) red chili flakes (optional)

In a large pot of boiling salted water, cook fettuccine for 8 minutes or until pasta is almost tender. Add shrimp, zucchini and red pepper to pot. Return to a boil. Reduce heat and cook for 3 minutes or until shrimp are pink and pasta is tender but firm. Drain.

Turn pasta back into pan. Stir in pesto, cheese and chili flakes if using. Divide between two serving dishes.

Makes 2 servings.

Presto Pesto

Pesto adds marvellous flavour to many dishes, from pizza to stir-frys. Traditionally made with basil, more recently, cilantro, mint and a variety of other greens have been used for variety.

1 cup (250 mL) packed basil or spinach leaves

1 clove garlic, chopped

1 tbsp (15 mL) pine nuts or walnuts

1 tbsp (15 mL) olive oil

3 tbsp (45 mL) grated Parmesan cheese

Process basil, garlic and pine nuts in a small food processor until finely chopped. Add olive oil, pulsing until blended. Stir in cheese.

Makes about 1/4 cup (50 mL).

+ Sautéed Spinach

A quick way to enhance the sweet flavour of spinach.

1 tbsp (15 mL) olive oil

1 clove garlic, chopped

8 oz (250 g) fresh spinach, torn into pieces (about 6 cups/1.5 L)

1 tsp (5 mL) lemon juice

In a medium skillet, heat olive oil over medium heat. Add garlic and cook for 30 seconds or until just starting to brown. Add spinach, tossing to coat. Cover and cook for 3 minutes or just until wilted. Stir in lemon juice before serving.

PER SERVING OF
MAIN DISH

Amount	% Daily Value
Calories 569	
Fat 14g	22%
Saturated 3.5g	18%
Monounsaturated 5.4g	
Polyunsaturated 2.5g	
Sodium 364mg	15%
Carbohydrate 70g	23%
Fibre 4g	16%
Protein 40g	
Calcium 246mg	22%

Salmon with Dijon and Sesame Glaze 📹

Preparation Time: 5 minutes Cook Time: 10 minutes

Simple and elegant, just a few ingredients combine to create a splendid gourmet dish. The mild mustard sauce enhanced with the flavour of sesame adds an exciting dimension to salmon or any firm-fleshed fish.

1 tbsp (15 mL) Dijon mustard
1 tsp (5 mL) honey
1/4 tsp (1 mL) sesame oil
2 salmon fillets, about 4 oz
 (125 g) each
1 tsp (5 mL) toasted sesame
 seeds (see page 40 for toasting
 instructions)

Preheat oven to 425°F (220°C). In a small dish, combine mustard, honey and sesame oil.

 Place fish in small flat baking dish. Brush fish with mustard mixture and sprinkle with sesame seeds. Bake for 10 to 12 minutes or until fish flakes easily when tested with a fork.

Makes 2 servings.

+ Rapini with Lemon and Shallots 📹

Olive oil and a touch of lemon enhance the pungent taste of this highly nutritious relative of broccoli.

1 tbsp (15 mL) olive oil
1 shallot, chopped
Grated zest of 1 lemon
1 tbsp (15 mL) lemon juice
2 cups (500 mL) rapini, cut into
 1/2-inch (1 cm) pieces
Salt and ground black pepper

In a large saucepan, heat olive oil over medium-high heat. Add shallot and cook for 2 minutes or until soft. Add lemon zest, lemon juice and rapini. Cover and cook for 1 minute or just until tender. Add salt and pepper to taste.

+ Herbed Whole Wheat Couscous 📹

A quick side dish nicely complements fish or grilled chicken. Look for whole wheat couscous in natural food stores.

3/4 cup (175 mL) low-sodium broth
1 green onion, sliced
1/2 cup (125 mL) whole wheat
 couscous
1 tbsp (15 mL) chopped fresh parsley

In a small saucepan, bring broth and green onion to a boil. Stir in couscous and parsley. Let stand for 5 minutes before serving

PER SERVING OF MAIN DISH	
Amount	**% Daily Value**
Calories 183	
Fat 8g	12%
Saturated 1.3g	7%
Monounsaturated 2.8g	
Polyunsaturated 3.4g	
Sodium 62mg	3%
Carbohydrate 3g	1%
Fibre 0g	0%
Protein 23g	
Calcium 15mg	1%

PER SERVING WITH SIDE DISHES	
Amount	**% Daily Value**
Calories 446	
Fat 16g	25%
Saturated 2.4g	12%
Monounsaturated 7.9g	
Polyunsaturated 4.1g	
Sodium 112mg	5%
Carbohydrate 43g	14%
Fibre 4g	16%
Protein 32g	
Calcium 93mg	8%

Grilled Trout with Fresh Dill and Chives

Preparation Time: 5 minutes Cook Time: 5 minutes

Trout and salmon are close relatives and both are rich in heart-healthy omega-3s. Each has its own unique rich, succulent flavour needing just a few simple ingredients to create a superb gourmet dish. Fortunately, trout is becoming more readily available with the development of more environmentally friendly farming practices.

2 tbsp (25 mL) chopped fresh chives
  or green onions
1 tbsp (15 mL) chopped fresh dill or
  1 tsp (5 mL) dried dillweed
Grated zest of 1/2 lemon
2 trout or salmon fillets, about 4 oz
  (125 g) each
1 tsp (5 mL) olive oil
1/2 lemon cut in wedges

Preheat grill to medium-hot. In a small bowl, combine chives, dill and lemon zest. Brush flesh side of fillets with olive oil and place fillets skin side down on grill. Spoon chive mixture over top of each fillet, close lid and grill until fish flakes easily when tested with a fork, about 5 minutes depending on thickness.

Makes 2 servings.

Salmon and Trout, Jewels of Canadian Cuisine

Omega-3 fatty acids, known to foster cardiovascular health, are a bonus in this meal. The omega-3s present in sardines, salmon, trout and other fish may reduce the likelihood of blood clotting and lessen the risk of a heart attack. Eating fish once or twice a week is a wise choice. Featuring salmon or trout twice a month creates an easy culinary delight.

+ Mandarin Orange Salad

Add spinach to torn greens for extra flavour and nutrients. Orange pieces with an orange-based vinaigrette completes the salad.

2 tbsp (25 mL) orange juice
1 tbsp (15 mL) white wine vinegar
1 tbsp (15 mL) canola oil
1 tsp (5 mL) lemon juice
1/2 tsp (2 mL) granulated sugar
Salt and ground black pepper
2 cups (500 mL) assorted torn greens
1 cup (250 mL) torn fresh spinach
1/2 cup (125 mL) mandarin orange
  pieces
2 thin slices sweet onion

In a small bowl, whisk together orange juice, vinegar, oil, lemon juice, sugar and salt and pepper to taste. Set aside.
  In a salad bowl, combine greens and spinach. Toss with dressing and garnish with mandarin orange pieces and sweet onion slices.

+ Lemon Rice

A new twist on the traditional lemon served with fish.

1 cup (250 mL) chicken broth
½ cup (125 mL) long grain rice
Grated zest of 1 lemon
Chopped fresh or dried dill

In a small saucepan, bring broth to a boil. Stir in rice. Reduce heat, cover and simmer for 15 to 20 minutes or until liquid is absorbed. Stir in lemon zest and a bit of dill.

+ Broccoli with Sun-Dried Tomatoes

Sun-dried tomatoes add a unique flavour to broccoli.

2 cups (500 mL) broccoli florets
1 tsp (5 mL) olive oil
1 clove garlic, minced
1 sun-dried tomato, thinly sliced

In a small saucepan, steam broccoli for 5 minutes or just until tender-crisp. Meanwhile, in a small microwave-safe dish, place olive oil and garlic. Microwave on 100% power for 30 seconds or until garlic is soft. Add sun-dried tomato. Toss with broccoli.

PER SERVING OF MAIN DISH	
Amount	**% Daily Value**
Calories 159	
Fat 6g	9%
Saturated 1.0g	5%
Monounsaturated 2.8g	
Polyunsaturated 1.6g	
Sodium 31mg	1%
Carbohydrate 3g	1%
Fibre 1g	4%
Protein 24g	
Calcium 96mg	9%

PER SERVING WITH SIDE DISHES	
Amount	**% Daily Value**
Calories 538	
Fat 18g	28%
Saturated 2.3g	12%
Monounsaturated 9.5g	
Polyunsaturated 4.4g	
Sodium 479mg	20%
Carbohydrate 65g	22%
Fibre 6g	24%
Protein 34g	
Calcium 188mg	17%

Tilapia with Zucchini and Tomatoes 📹

Preparation Time: 10 minutes Cook Time: 15 minutes

A savoury mixture of zucchini and tomatoes adds zest to tilapia, a mild-flavoured fish. The fillets steam quickly and are ready for your plate in just minutes.

2 tsp (10 mL) olive oil
1 small onion, chopped
1 clove garlic, chopped
1 small zucchini, thinly sliced
1 plum tomato, diced
1 1/2 tsp (7 mL) chopped fresh
  oregano, or 1/2 tsp (2 mL) dried
2 tilapia or other fish fillets such as
  sole or cod, about 4 oz (125 g) each

In a medium skillet with a tight-fitting lid, heat oil over medium heat. Add onion and garlic and cook for 3 minutes or until onion is opaque. Add zucchini and tomato and cook 5 minutes or until softened. Stir in oregano.

Lay fillets on top of vegetables. Cover skillet, reduce heat to medium low, and boil gently about 5 minutes or just until fish will flake easily with a fork.

Makes 2 servings.

+ Bulgur with Olives and Lemon

Olive oil and a few olives add interest to bulgur, ready in just a few minutes.

1 tbsp (15 mL) olive oil
1 clove garlic, minced
3/4 cup (175 mL) water
Dash salt
1/2 cup (125 mL) bulgur
Grated zest of 1 lemon
8 pited black olives, chopped
2 tbsp (25 mL) chopped fresh parsley

In a small saucepan, heat olive oil over medium heat. Add garlic and cook for 2 minutes or until soft and fragrant. Add water and salt. Bring to a boil. Stir in bulgur, lemon zest and black olives. Remove from heat and let stand for 10 minutes. Stir in parsley.

+ Peas and Kohlrabi Combo

Kohlrabi adds interesting texture and a mild taste, which nicely complements sweet green peas.

3 tbsp (45 mL) water
1 cup (250 mL) diced kohlrabi
1 cup (250 mL) frozen small peas
2 tsp (10 mL) butter
Salt and ground black pepper
Chopped fresh herbs (thyme,
  oregano, parsley)

In a small saucepan, bring water to a boil over high heat. Add kohlrabi. Cover, return to a boil and cook for 4 minutes. Add peas. Return to a boil and cook for 3 minutes or until peas and kohlrabi are tender. Drain and stir in butter and salt and ground black pepper to taste. Add a sprinkling of any fresh herb you have on hand.

PER SERVING OF MAIN DISH	
Amount	% Daily Value
Calories 192	
Fat 6g	9%
Saturated 1.0g	5%
Monounsaturated 3.7g	
Polyunsaturated 0.9g	
Sodium 106mg	4%
Carbohydrate 11g	4%
Fibre 2g	8%
Protein 23g	
Calcium 54mg	5%

PER SERVING WITH SIDE DISHES	
Amount	% Daily Value
Calories 498	
Fat 19g	29%
Saturated 4.6g	23%
Monounsaturated 11g	
Polyunsaturated 2.1g	
Sodium 358mg	15%
Carbohydrate 53g	18%
Fibre 12g	48%
Protein 33g	
Calcium 118mg	11%

Bulgur

Bulgur is a nutritious staple common in the Middle East that is made from the whole kernel of wheat. Since it is precooked, it needs only a few minutes standing in a hot liquid before serving. Cracked wheat is also made from the whole wheat kernel, but has not been precooked and requires a much longer preparation time.

Quick Fish and Vegetables En Papillote

Preparation Time: 10 minutes Cook Time: 10 minutes

En papillote refers to food baked inside a wrapping of parchment or foil. The flavours blend beautifully, and the packages cook quickly in a microwave oven. Let each person unfold their package and savour the wonderful aroma.

1 carrot, very thinly sliced
2 fish fillets, such as sole or flounder, about 4 oz (125 g) each
4 green onions, sliced
4 mushrooms, sliced
1 small zucchini, sliced
1 tbsp (15 mL) fresh lemon juice
2 tsp (10 mL) olive or canola oil
1 tsp (5 mL) chopped fresh thyme, or ¼ tsp (1 mL) dried
Salt and ground black pepper

If using oven, preheat to 400°F (200°C). Cut two sheets of parchment paper into rectangles about 12 x 15 in (30 x 37 cm).

Place half the carrots in a mound in the centre of each rectangle. Layer half the fish over each mound. Cover with half the green onions, mushrooms and zucchini.

In a small bowl, whisk together the lemon juice, oil, thyme, salt and pepper as desired. Drizzle over vegetables and fish.

Bring short sides of paper together, folding edges twice to seal tightly. Roll remaining ends tightly together to seal.

Place on a microwave-safe plate and microwave on 100% power for 6 minutes or until fish flakes easily with a fork and vegetables are tender. After testing, refold the packet and place on a plate for each person.

Makes 2 servings.

Note: Papillotes wrapped in foil can be baked for 25 minutes or until fish flakes easily with a fork and vegetables are tender.

+ Quick Baked Tomatoes

Baking tomatoes with bread crumbs and cheese produces the intense flavour of roasted vegetables without the added oil.

2 medium tomatoes
2 tsp (10 mL) Italian-flavoured dry bread crumbs
2 tsp (10 mL) grated Parmesan cheese

If you are using an oven instead of microwave, preheat to 400°F (200°C). Cut tomatoes in half. Set in a flat glass baking dish. Sprinkle each with half the bread crumbs and half the cheese. Microwave on 100% power for 2 minutes or bake for 15 minutes or until tomatoes are just soft.

PER SERVING OF MAIN DISHES	
Amount	**% Daily Value**
Calories 190	
Fat 6g	9%
Saturated 1.0g	5%
Monounsaturated 3.6g	
Polyunsaturated 0.9g	
Sodium 134mg	6%
Carbohydrate 10g	3%
Fibre 3g	12%
Protein 24g	
Calcium 69mg	6%

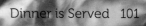

+ Couscous with Lemon and Herbs

Couscous with a hint of lemon and fresh herbs is a perfect accompaniment to fish. Garnish with currants or sunflower seeds for added texture and flavour.

1 tsp (5 mL) canola oil
1 shallot, minced
³/₄ cup (175 mL) sodium-reduced chicken broth
¹/₂ cup (125 mL) couscous
Grated zest of ¹/₂ lemon
1 tbsp (15 mL) chopped fresh parsley, basil, oregano, thyme or rosemary

In a small saucepan, heat oil over medium heat. Add shallot and cook for 2 minutes or until soft. Add broth. Bring to a boil and stir in couscous and lemon zest. Remove from heat, cover and let stand for 5 minutes. Stir in herbs.

+ Spinach Sprout Salad

Fresh sprouts and sesame seeds garnish this Japanese-inspired salad.

2 tbsp (25 mL) rice vinegar
2 tbsp (25 mL) pineapple or orange juice
1 tsp (5 mL) granulated sugar
1 tsp (5 mL) sodium-reduced soy sauce
¹/₂ tsp (2 mL) sesame oil
Ground black pepper
2 cups (500 mL) torn fresh spinach leaves
¹/₂ cup (125 mL) fresh bean sprouts
1 tbsp (15 mL) toasted sesame seeds (see page 40 for toasting instructions)

In a small bowl, whisk together rice vinegar, juice, sugar, soy sauce, sesame oil and pepper to taste. Set aside.

In a salad bowl, combine spinach and bean sprouts. Toss with dressing and sprinkle with sesame seeds.

Couscous

Couscous is a perfect food for two since it requires little cooking and is easy to prepare in small quantities. A staple of North African cuisine, couscous is made from semolina, the coarsely ground endosperm of durum wheat. It is similar to pasta, although couscous is usually sold precooked. The traditional way to prepare it is to steam it in the top of a special pot called a *couscoussière* while pieces of meat and vegetables cook below. This method produces couscous that is the most fluffy, but stirring it into boiling broth works just fine.

PER SERVING WITH SIDE DISHES	
Amount	% Daily Value
Calories 508	
Fat 14g	22%
Saturated 2.1g	11%
Monounsaturated 6.7g	
Polyunsaturated 3.4g	
Sodium 547mg	23%
Carbohydrate 64g	21%
Fibre 8g	32%
Protein 36g	
Calcium 207mg	19%

Edamame, Corn and Red Pepper Stir-Fry

Preparation Time: 10 minutes Cook Time: 10 minutes

Green soybeans, known as edamame, are becomingly increasingly favoured on Canadian dinner plates for their nutritional benefits as well as their nutty taste. Adding them to some sautéed vegetables makes a quick one-dish meal. Serve with slices of a whole grain loaf.

2 to 3 slices bacon
2 cloves garlic, minced
1 sweet red pepper, diced
1/2 jalapeño pepper, minced
1/2 cup (125 mL) chopped celery
1/3 cup (75 mL) chopped red onion
1 1/2 cups (375 mL) frozen corn
3/4 cup (175 mL) frozen shelled
  edamame
3 tbsp (45 mL) sherry
2 tbsp (25 mL) chopped fresh parsley
Salt and ground black pepper

In a large nonstick skillet, cook bacon over medium-high heat until crisp. Remove from pan and reserve 1 tbsp (15 mL) bacon drippings in pan. Crumble bacon. Set aside.

Add garlic, red pepper, jalapeño pepper, celery and onion. Cook for 2 minutes, stirring frequently or until soft. Stir in corn, edamame and sherry. Bring to a boil. Reduce heat and cook for 3 minutes or until corn and edamame are cooked and liquid is evaporated.

Remove from heat. Stir in reserved bacon, parsley and salt and pepper to taste.

Makes 2 servings.

+ Carrot, Apple and Horseradish Salad

Horseradish adds interesting flavour to a simple apple and carrot salad.

2 tbsp (25 mL) plain yogurt
2 tbsp (25 mL) mayonnaise
1 tsp (5 mL) prepared horseradish
1/2 tsp (2 mL) granulated sugar
2 carrots, grated
1 apple, peeled and grated
1 tbsp (15 mL) chopped fresh parsley

In a medium bowl, combine yogurt, mayonnaise, horseradish and sugar. Stir in carrots, apple and parsley.

PER SERVING WITH SIDE DISHES	
Amount	% Daily Value
Calories 482	
Fat 19g	29%
Saturated 3.3g	17%
Monounsaturated 8.2g	
Polyunsaturated 6.5g	
Sodium 548mg	23%
Carbohydrate 60g	20%
Fibre 10g	40%
Protein 20g	
Calcium 198mg	18%

PER SERVING OF MAIN DISH	
Amount	% Daily Value
Calories 303	
Fat 7g	11%
Saturated 1.4g	7%
Monounsaturated 2.0g	
Polyunsaturated 2.6g	
Sodium 395mg	16%
Carbohydrate 41g	14%
Fibre 7g	28%
Protein 18g	
Calcium 137mg	12%

Florentine Fillets with Poppy Seeds

Preparation Time: 5 minutes Cook Time: 10 minutes

Poppy seeds make an interesting topping for fish fillets served on a bed of orange-infused spinach. Use any lean fish such as tilapia, sole, grouper or perch.

1 bunch fresh spinach, about 10 oz (280 g)
2 skinless fish fillets such as tilapia or sole, about 4 oz (125 g) each
1 tbsp (15 mL) plain yogurt
1 tbsp (15 mL) poppy seeds
1 tbsp (15 mL) olive oil
1/4 cup (50 mL) orange juice

Place rinsed spinach in a microwave-safe container. Microwave on 100% power for 1 to 2 minutes or until wilted. Drain and set aside.

Coat top of each fish fillet with yogurt. Sprinkle with seeds.

In a small skillet, heat oil over medium heat. Carefully place fillets seed side down in pan and cook for 2 minutes or until edges of fillets begin to curl. Turn and cook another 2 minutes or just until fish flakes easily with a fork. Remove from pan and set aside.

Add orange juice to pan, bring to a boil and simmer for 3 to 5 minutes or until juice is reduced by two-thirds. Add spinach and stir to coat. Divide spinach onto two plates and top with fish.

Makes 2 servings.

+ Red Cabbage with Caraway Seeds

Currant jelly and caraway seeds add interesting flavour to steamed red cabbage.

2 cups (500 mL) sliced red cabbage
1 tsp (5 mL) red currant jelly
1/4 tsp (1 mL) caraway seeds

In a saucepan with water and a steamer rack, steam cabbage for 5 minutes or until tender. Remove, drain if necessary, and toss with jelly and seeds.

+ Squash Purée with Lime

A hint of lime gives squash a winning flavour.

2 cups (500 mL) peeled cubed butternut squash
2 tbsp (25 mL) lime juice
1 tbsp (15 mL) olive oil
1 tbsp (15 mL) honey
Grated nutmeg

In a small steamer, steam squash for 10 minutes or until very tender. Transfer to a bowl and mash until smooth. Stir in lime juice, olive oil and honey. Add nutmeg to taste.

PER SERVING OF MAIN DISH	
Amount	% Daily Value
Calories 235	
Fat 11g	17%
Saturated 1.6g	8%
Monounsaturated 5.6g	
Polyunsaturated 2.4g	
Sodium 209mg	9%
Carbohydrate 10g	3%
Fibre 4g	16%
Protein 26g	
Calcium 234mg	21%

PER SERVING WITH SIDE DISHES	
Amount	% Daily Value
Calories 452	
Fat 18g	28%
Saturated 2.6g	13%
Monounsaturated 10.7g	
Polyunsaturated 3.3g	
Sodium 278mg	12%
Carbohydrate 50g	17%
Fibre 10g	40%
Protein 31g	
Calcium 385mg	35%

SPEEDY TOPPINGS FOR PASTA

Preparation Time: 10 minutes Cook Time: 15 to 20 minutes

Here's a quartet of quickly prepared sauces to serve with your favourite pasta. Each recipe, served with 4 to 6 ounces (125 to 170 g) pasta, is enough for two people. These sauces are also excellent on top of cooked rice or spaghetti squash. A sprinkle of freshly grated Parmesan cheese adds a finishing touch and a green salad is the perfect companion.

Turkey Italian Pasta Topping

A few vegetables and ground turkey blend wonderfully into a fresh-tasting sauce with Italian flavours. Another time, replace the ground turkey with a can of tuna.

1 tsp (5 mL) canola oil
1 small onion, chopped
1 clove garlic, minced
6 oz (170 g) lean ground turkey or
    chicken
1 small zucchini, chopped
1/2 sweet green pepper, diced
2 large tomatoes, peeled and
    chopped or 1 cup (250 mL) canned
1 tbsp (15 mL) chopped fresh basil or
    1 tsp (5 mL) dried
1 tbsp (15 mL) chopped fresh oregano
    or 1 tsp (5 mL) dried
1/4 tsp (1 mL) granulated sugar
1/8 tsp (1/2 mL) salt

In a medium nonstick skillet, heat oil over medium-high heat. Add onion and garlic. Cook, stirring often, for 5 minutes until onion is soft. Add turkey. Cook, stirring, until no pink remains.

Add zucchini, green pepper, tomatoes, basil, oregano, sugar and salt. Bring to a boil. Reduce heat and simmer, uncovered, stirring occasionally for 15 minutes or until liquid is thickened.

Makes 2 servings.

PER SERVING WITH 2.5 oz (70 g) DRY PASTA AND 1 tbsp (15 mL) GRATED PARMESAN	
Amount	% Daily Value
Calories 506	
Fat 13g	20%
Saturated 3.5g	18%
Monounsaturated 5.0g	
Polyunsaturated 2.7g	
Sodium 342mg	14%
Carbohydrate 69g	23%
Fibre 6g	24%
Protein 29g	
Calcium 138mg	13%

Fresh Tomato Pasta Topping with Tuna ▭◁

When sun-ripened tomatoes and zucchini are in season, combine them with fresh herbs for an ambrosial pasta sauce. This delicious sauce also goes nicely with spaghetti squash.

1 tsp (5 mL) canola oil
1 small onion, chopped
1 clove garlic, minced
2 large tomatoes, peeled and
   chopped
1 stalk celery, chopped
1 small zucchini, chopped
1 tsp (5 mL) lemon juice
1/4 tsp (1 mL) granulated sugar
1 tbsp (15 mL) chopped fresh basil or
   1 tsp (5 mL) dried
1 tsp (5 mL) chopped fresh oregano
   or 1/4 tsp (1 mL) dried
1/8 tsp (1/2 mL) salt
1/8 tsp (1/2 mL) ground black pepper
1 can (6 oz/170 g) water-packed tuna,
   drained

In a nonstick skillet, heat oil over medium heat. Cook onion and garlic until tender, about 5 minutes. Add tomatoes, celery, zucchini, lemon juice, sugar, herbs, and salt and pepper to taste.. Bring to a boil. Reduce heat and cook until liquid is thickened, about 15 minutes, stirring occasionally.

   Break tuna into chunks and add to sauce. Heat to serving temperature.

Makes 2 servings.

Tuna Facts

In North America five species of tuna are caught commercially. Albacore is the only one that carries the name "white tuna" on the label. It commands the highest price. "Light" on the label refers to species of tuna that are light in colour such as skipjack, yellowfin and bluefin. "Light" does not give an indication of its fat or calorie content. To cut down on calories, look for water-packed tuna, which offers about a 30 per cent calorie saving over the oil-packed.

PER SERVING WITH
2.5 oz (70 g) DRY PASTA
AND 1 tbsp (15 mL)
GRATED PARMESAN

Amount	% Daily Value
Calories 437	
Fat 6g	9%
Saturated 1.6g	8%
Monounsaturated 2.2g	
Polyunsaturated 1.6g	
Sodium 481mg	20%
Carbohydrate 66g	22%
Fibre 5g	20%
Protein 29g	
Calcium 127mg	12%

Red Lentil Pasta Topping 🎥

Red lentils cook to a thick purée making a luscious sauce for topping pasta. This version is based on the earthy flavours of Italian sauces. Add a bit of cooked sausage, chopped ham or a few anchovy fillets if you have them on hand.

1 tsp (5 mL) olive or canola oil
1 onion, finely chopped
1 clove garlic, minced
1 1/4 cups (300 mL) low-sodium chicken or vegetable broth
1/3 cup (75 mL) dried red lentils, rinsed
2 tbsp (25 mL) tomato paste
1/4 cup (50 mL) finely chopped fresh basil or 1 tbsp (15 mL) dried
1/4 cup (50 mL) finely chopped fresh parsley, or 1 tbsp (15 mL) dried
1/4 cup (50 mL) chopped black olives (optional)
1 tbsp (15 mL) drained capers, rinsed
Salt and ground black pepper

In a medium saucepan, heat oil over medium heat. Add onion and garlic. Cook for 5 minutes or until soft.

Add broth, lentils and tomato paste. Bring to a boil. Reduce heat, cover and simmer for 15 minutes or until lentils are very soft.

Add basil, parsley, olives (if using) and capers. Add salt and pepper to taste.

Makes 2 servings.

Broccoli and Ham Pasta Topping

Keep this recipe in mind the next time you have leftover baked ham. Evaporated milk makes a rich creamy sauce with double the calcium of regular milk. Remember, ham brings a sizeable measure of sodium, so reduce the amount of ham if you need to limit this mineral in your diet.

3 cups (750 mL) small broccoli florets
2 tsp (10 mL) canola oil
1 leek, white and light green parts only, thinly sliced
1 cup (250 mL) sliced mushrooms
3/4 cup (175 mL) 2% evaporated milk
1/4 cup (50 mL) dry white wine
1 tbsp (15 mL) all-purpose flour
1/3 cup (75 mL) chopped cooked ham, about 2 oz (60 g)
1 1/2 tsp (7 mL) chopped fresh basil or 1/2 tsp (2 mL) dried
Salt and ground black pepper

In a large pot of boiling water, cook broccoli for 5 minutes, or until tender-crisp. Drain and set aside.

Meanwhile, in a nonstick skillet, heat oil over medium-high heat. Add leek and mushrooms. Cook for 3 minutes or until slightly soft.

In a small bowl, whisk together milk, wine and flour. Stir into skillet. Bring to a boil, stirring constantly. Cook for 1 minute or until thickened and bubbly. Stir in ham, basil and broccoli. Cook until sauce just returns to a boil. Add salt and pepper to taste.

Makes 2 servings

RED LENTIL PASTA TOPPING	
PER SERVING WITH 2.5 oz (70 g) DRY PASTA AND 1 tbsp (15 mL) GRATED PARMESAN	
Amount	**% Daily Value**
Calories 488	
Fat 7g	11%
Saturated 1.9g	10%
Monounsaturated 2.4g	
Polyunsaturated 0.9g	
Sodium 257mg	11%
Carbohydrate 84g	28%
Fibre 7g	28%
Protein 25g	
Calcium 145mg	13%

BROCCOLI AND HAM	
PER SERVING WITH 2.5 oz (70 g) DRY PASTA AND 1 tbsp (15 mL) GRATED PARMESAN	
Amount	**% Daily Value**
Calories 582	
Fat 12g	18%
Saturated 3.2g	16%
Monounsaturated 4.6g	
Polyunsaturated 2.5g	
Sodium 554mg	23%
Carbohydrate 88g	29%
Fibre 8g	32%
Protein 30g	
Calcium 462mg	42%

Thai-Style Edamame and Veggies

Preparation Time: 15 minutes Cook Time: 15 minutes

The classic Thai dish, paht si-yu, was the inspiration for this recipe. Similar to pad Thai, the flavours wonderfully enhance green soybeans and cauliflower for a zesty one-dish meal. True Thai cooking uses much more fish sauce than is in this recipe. Fish sauce is very high in salt and we were surprised to discover that Thai rice-stick noodles also contain a large amount. So to keep the sodium in check, we have used regular pasta and reduced the amount of fish sauce, getting good flavour from other ingredients.

4 oz (120 g) linguine or fettuccine
1 tbsp (15 mL) balsamic vinegar
1 tsp (5 mL) fish sauce
1 tsp (5 mL) sodium-reduced soy
  sauce
1/4 tsp (1 mL) ground black pepper
1 tbsp (15 mL) canola oil
1 onion, diced
1 tbsp (15 mL) chopped garlic
2 cups (500 mL) small cauliflower
  florets
3/4 cup (175 mL) frozen shelled
  edamame, about 4 oz (125 g)
1 small sweet red pepper, chopped
1/2 cup (125 mL) low-sodium chicken
  broth
3 cups (750 mL) chopped Swiss chard
  leaves, about 4 oz (125 g)

In a large pot of boiling salted water, cook linguine for 8 to 10 minutes or just until tender yet firm. Drain and rinse with hot water. Drain and set aside.

Meanwhile, in a small bowl, combine vinegar, fish sauce, soy sauce and pepper. Set aside.

In a large nonstick skillet or wok, heat oil over medium heat. Add onion and garlic. Cook for 2 minutes, stirring constantly. Add cauliflower, edamame, red pepper and broth. Bring to a boil. Reduce heat, cover and simmer for 4 minutes or until vegetables are tender, stirring frequently.

Add chard and soy sauce mixture. Cook for 2 minutes longer. Stir in linguine and toss until well mixed.

Makes 2 servings.

PER SERVING OF MAIN DISH	
Amount	% Daily Value
Calories 472	
Fat 13g	20%
Saturated 1.4g	7%
Monounsaturated 5.0g	
Polyunsaturated 4.7g	
Sodium 502mg	21%
Carbohydrate 72g	24%
Fibre 9g	36%
Protein 22g	
Calcium 192mg	17%

Fish Sauce

Fish sauce is ubiquitous in Thai cooking. Made from small salted fish such as anchovies, it is a pungent salty liquid used throughout southeast Asian countries from Vietnam, Laos and Cambodia to Burma (Myanmar) and Malaysia. Look for it in the Asian section of most supermarkets. There is no substitute, but if you can't find it, increase the amount of soy sauce. But beware, both sauces are very high in sodium.

Barley Lentil Bake with Mushrooms

Preparation Time: 10 minutes Cook Time: 70 minutes

Barley and quick-cooking red lentils team up to make a delicious and satisfying meat-alternative that is high in fibre and an excellent source of vitamins A and C, folate and iron. As a colourful accompaniment with poultry or meat, this bake will serve four people.

1 tsp (5 mL) canola oil
1 cup (250 mL) sliced mushrooms
2 carrots, chopped
1 stalk celery, chopped
1 small onion, chopped
1/3 cup (75 mL) pot or pearl barley, rinsed
1/3 cup (75 mL) dried red lentils, rinsed
1 1/3 cup (325 mL) sodium-reduced chicken broth
2 tbsp (25 mL) tomato paste
1 1/2 tsp (7 mL) chopped fresh oregano or 1/2 tsp (2 mL) dried
1/4 tsp (1 mL) ground black pepper
Salt

Preheat oven to 350°F (180°C). In a small nonstick skillet, heat oil over medium-high heat. Add mushrooms, carrots, celery and onion. Cook for 8 minutes or until vegetables are soft. Transfer to a 1-quart (1 L) casserole dish.

Stir in barley, lentils, broth, tomato paste, oregano, pepper and salt if desired.

Bake for 1 hour if using pearl barley or 1 1/4 hours if using pot barley, or until liquid is absorbed and barley is tender.

Makes 2 servings.

+ Orange Date Salad with Honey-Mustard Dressing

Orange, dates and a sweet mustard dressing combine beautifully for a refreshing salad.

1 tbsp (15 mL) canola oil
1 tbsp (15 mL) white wine vinegar
1 tbsp (15 mL) honey
1/2 tsp (2 mL) Dijon mustard
Salt and ground black pepper
2 1/2 cups (625 mL) torn assorted lettuces
1/2 cup (125 mL) torn spinach leaves
1 seedless orange, peeled and sliced
2 tbsp (25 mL) chopped dates
2 tbsp (25 mL) whole wheat croutons
1 tbsp (15 mL) toasted sesame seeds (see page 24 for toasting instructions)

In a small bowl, whisk together oil, vinegar, honey, mustard and salt and pepper to taste. Set aside.

In a salad bowl, place lettuces, spinach and orange slices. Toss with dressing and garnish with dates, croutons and sesame seeds.

PER SERVING OF MAIN DISH	
Amount	% Daily Value
Calories 338	
Fat 4g	6%
Saturated 0.5g	3%
Monounsaturated 1.6g	
Polyunsaturated 1.4g	
Sodium 464mg	19%
Carbohydrate 63g	21%
Fibre 10g	40%
Protein 17g	
Calcium 95mg	9%

PER SERVING WITH SIDE DISHES	
Amount	% Daily Value
Calories 610	
Fat 16g	25%
Saturated 1.7g	9%
Monounsaturated 8.3g	
Polyunsaturated 4.9g	
Sodium 524mg	22%
Carbohydrate 105g	35%
Fibre 17g	68%
Protein 22g	
Calcium 239mg	22%

+ Broccoli with Yellow Peppers

A delightful colour combination for a favourite vegetable.

2 cups (500 mL) broccoli florets
¼ sweet yellow pepper, cut in slivers
1 tsp (5 mL) olive oil or butter

Steam broccoli with yellow pepper for 5 minutes or until just tender-crisp. Add olive oil or butter as desired.

Fresh Basil, Rapini and Tomato Pasta with Feta Cheese

Preparation Time: 10 minutes Cook Time: 10 minutes

This colourful pasta meal is brimming with healthful nutrients. Topped with feta, it makes a superb main dish. Use broccoli or any leafy green such as Swiss chard or kale to replace the rapini.

2 cups (500 mL) whole wheat fusili or
  rotini pasta, about 5 oz (150 g)
1 tbsp (15 mL) olive oil
3 cloves garlic, minced
6 plum tomatoes, peeled and
  chopped, about 12 oz (375 g)
4 cups (1 L) coarsely chopped rapini
6 leaves fresh basil, chopped, or 1 tsp
  (5 mL) dried
1/2 cup (125 mL) crumbled feta cheese

In a large pot of boiling salted water, cook pasta for 10 minutes or until tender but firm. Drain and rinse with hot water.

Meanwhile, in a large skillet, heat oil over medium heat. Add garlic and cook for 1 minute or until lightly browned. Add tomatoes. Bring to a boil and cook for 2 minutes or until soft, stirring frequently. Stir in rapini and basil, return to boil, cover and boil gently for 3 to 5 minutes, stirring occasionally, or until rapini is tender.

Divide pasta into two bowls, spoon tomato mixture over and top with cheese.

Makes 2 servings.

+ On the Grill

While the main dish cooks, heat up the grill for an easy side of chicken or fish.

2 pieces chicken or fish, about 4 oz
  (125 g) each
1/2 tsp (2 mL) barbeque or other
  basting sauce

Preheat grill to hot. Brush chicken or fish with sauce and grill until an instant-read thermometer reads 165° (74°C).

PER SERVING OF MAIN DISH		
Amount		**% Daily Value**
Calories 494		
Fat 17g		26%
Saturated 7.0g		35%
Monounsaturated 7.2g		
Polyunsaturated 1.4g		
Sodium 472mg		20%
Carbohydrate 72g		24%
Fibre 11g		44%
Protein 22g		
Calcium 332mg		30%

PER SERVING WITH SIDE DISHES		
Amount		**% Daily Value**
Calories 619		
Fat 19g		29%
Saturated 7.4g		37%
Monounsaturated 7.7g		
Polyunsaturated 1.9g		
Sodium 551mg		23%
Carbohydrate 72g		24%
Fibre 11g		44%
Protein 47g		
Calcium 345mg		31%

Rapini

Also called broccoli rabe, rapini is a close relative to broccoli. The entire plant is edible with the leaves having a stronger taste than the stems and buds. Like its cabbage relatives, rapini is an excellent source of vitamins and powerful phytochemicals, which offer many health benefits.

SATISFYING SOUPS

Our soups come in many moods. Some can be a pleasing prelude to a special meal. Others, like Mixed Mushroom Soup with Fresh Thyme and Leeks (page 134), are perfect luncheon companions to sandwiches or crackers and cheese. The hearty Soup with Lentils, Fresh Herbs and Kale (page 130) yearns for wholesome bread and a fruit yogurt to turn itself into a satisfying feast.

These soup selections were designed as avenues for you to access a wide variety of vegetables and to become better acquainted with the world of legumes. In some recipes we have married a few of the more robust flavours with the smooth taste of milk. In others, we have highlighted distinctive ingredients. The result is a mix of stimulating flavour and a healthy blend of essential nutrients.

How much you fill that soup bowl depends on how you choose to feature soup as part of your meal. Our serving size suggestions are just that — suggestions. If you are looking for a taste-teaser, then go for only a three-quarter cup. But if you intend to anchor your meal with the soup, a double serving may well be in order. The nutritional analysis gives guidance on how to complete the meal. Keep in mind that 500 calories and choices from all the food groups are a good aim for a lunch or supper. And to keep sodium in check, look for low-sodium broth or make your own (page 129) with no added salt

These soups appeal to a range of tastes — from the traditional Fagioli (page 138) to the more exotic flavour of Hot and Sour Soup (page 126). Search for the ones that suit your mood — then sit down and enjoy!

Quick Vegetable Egg-Drop Soup for One

Preparation Time: 5 minutes Cook Time: 10 minutes

Frozen vegetables add flavour to traditional Chinese egg-drop soup, ready in just ten minutes.

1 ½ cups (375 mL) low-sodium chicken broth

½ to 1 tsp (2 to 5 mL) sodium-reduced soy sauce

½ cup (125 mL) frozen peas and carrots or other mixed vegetables

¼ cup (50 mL) small pasta or noodles such as filini or orzo

1 egg, lightly beaten

1 green onion, sliced (optional)

Salt and ground black pepper

In a medium saucepan, bring broth and soy sauce to a boil. Add vegetables and noodles. Return to a boil. Reduce heat, cover and simmer, stirring frequently, for 5 minutes or until pasta is just tender.

Remove soup from heat and slowly pour egg into hot soup, stirring constantly as you pour. Add salt and pepper to taste. Ladle into bowl and garnish with green onion (if using).

Makes 1 serving, about 2 cups (500 mL).

PER SERVING	
Amount	**% Daily Value**
Calories 275	
Fat 8g	12%
Saturated 2.4g	12%
Monounsaturated 2.0g	
Polyunsaturated 1.0g	
Sodium 321mg	13%
Carbohydrate 33g	11%
Fibre 3g	12%
Protein 19g	
Calcium 62mg	6%

Soy Sauce

Widely used in Asian cooking, soy sauce is a dark, salty condiment made by fermenting soybeans, salt and roasted wheat or barley. It has many forms in China and Japan, ranging from thin light sauces to thicker, richer-flavoured dark ones. Japanese soy sauces, such as tamari, tend to be sweeter than those used in China. Sodium-reduced soy sauce is readily available, which helps to keep sodium in check although even this version is far from sodium-free. Soy sauce will keep for many months if stored in a cool, dark place.

Fresh Tomato Soup

Preparation Time: 10 minutes Cook Time: 20 minutes

Take advantage of fresh vine-ripened tomatoes to make this superb cream soup. Thickening the milk before adding the tomatoes is the secret to preventing the soup from curdling. If fresh tomatoes aren't available, use either diced canned tomatoes or tomato juice. Add leftover cooked rice to make a hearty variation.

2 tsp (10 mL) olive oil
2 tbsp (25 mL) finely chopped onion
2 tbsp (25 mL) finely chopped celery
2 tsp (10 mL) all-purpose flour
1 tsp (5 mL) chopped fresh basil or
   thyme or ¼ tsp (1 mL) dried
½ tsp (2 mL) granulated sugar
⅔ cup (150 mL) milk
2 cups (500 mL) peeled ripe
   tomatoes, finely diced, about 1 lb
   (500 g)
Salt and ground black pepper

In a large saucepan, heat oil over medium-low heat. Add onion and celery. Cook for 10 minutes or until very soft.

Stir in flour, basil and sugar. Gradually stir in milk. Bring to a boil, stirring constantly. Cook gently for 1 minute or until thickened and bubbly.

Stir in tomatoes. Return to boil, stirring frequently. Reduce heat and simmer for 5 minutes. If a smooth texture is desired, put soup through a food mill or strainer to remove seeds. Add salt and pepper to taste.

Makes 2 servings, about 1 ⅓ cups (325 mL) each.

TLC for Tomatoes

For peak flavour and to enhance the ripening process, store tomatoes at room temperature. To avoid the need for refrigeration, buy tomatoes at different stages of ripeness, remembering that fully ripe tomatoes will keep a day or two at room temperature.

PER SERVING	
Amount	% Daily Value
Calories 146	
Fat 7g	11%
Saturated 1.6g	8%
Monounsaturated 4.0g	
Polyunsaturated 0.7g	
Sodium 57mg	2%
Carbohydrate 18g	6%
Fibre 3g	12%
Protein 5g	
Calcium 112mg	10%

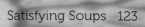

Gazpacho 🎥

Preparation Time: 15 minutes

Originating in southern Spain, this cold vegetable soup is wonderfully refreshing on a hot summer day. Traditionally, the vegetables were rubbed through a sieve, removing some of the seeds and pulp. Commercial tomato juice and the use of a blender make the job a lot easier. Although not traditional, beef broth adds a nice depth of flavour. For a spicier version, add a few drops hot pepper sauce.

1 ½ cup (375 mL) coarsely chopped ripe tomatoes, about 12 oz (350 g)
1 cup (250 mL) chopped seedless cucumber
2 tbsp (25 mL) finely chopped shallot or onion
½ sweet green pepper, chopped
1 clove garlic, crushed
1 cup (250 mL) water
¼ cup (50 mL) tomato paste
2 tbsp (25 mL) red wine vinegar
1 ½ tsp (7 mL) extra-virgin olive oil
½ tsp (2 mL) granulated sugar
½ tsp (2 mL) Worcestershire sauce
Salt and ground black pepper
Garnish: croutons, chopped tomatoes, cucumbers, green peppers and onions

In a food processor, combine tomatoes, cucumber, shallot, green pepper and garlic. Process until finely chopped. Transfer to a medium bowl.

Stir in water, tomato paste, vinegar, oil, sugar and Worcestershire. Add salt and pepper to taste. Chill until serving time to blend flavours.

Serve with the croutons and chopped vegetables presented in separate serving bowls to be added to the soup as desired.

Makes 2 servings, about 1 ¾ cups (425 mL) each.

A Touch of Sugar

Just a small amount of granulated sugar helps to cut the acidity in this soup. Keep this tip in mind for other foods that are very acidic.

Terrific Tomatoes

Evidence is mounting that tomato consumption reduces the risk of various cancers. The red pigment, lycopene, found mostly in tomato products such as juice, sauce or paste, is thought to be responsible for this effect. The body takes up the lycopene more readily from tomato products that have been cooked or heated.

PER SERVING	
Amount	% Daily Value
Calories 139	
Fat 5g	8%
Saturated 0.8g	4%
Monounsaturated 2.7g	
Polyunsaturated 0.6g	
Sodium 101mg	4%
Carbohydrate 22g	7%
Fibre 5g	20%
Protein 6g	
Calcium 42mg	4%

Hot and Sour Soup

Preparation Time: 10 minutes Cook Time: 10 minutes

This soup has a lively, robust flavour reminiscent of the Szechuan region of China. In smaller portions, it will arouse the appetite for a course to follow. Don't let the number of ingredients deter you. They cook together in only a few minutes.

1 boneless butterfly pork chop, about
   4 oz (125 g)
6 small brown or white mushrooms,
   cut into thin slices
1 carrot, grated
$1/3$ cup (75 mL) thinly sliced water
   chestnuts or bamboo shoots
2 tsp (10 mL) finely grated fresh
   ginger
3 cups (750 mL) low-sodium chicken
   broth
1 tbsp (15 mL) rice vinegar
1 $1/2$ tsp (7 mL) sodium-reduced soy
   sauce
$1/2$ tsp (2 mL) hot pepper sauce or
    1 $1/2$ tsp (7 mL) hot chili paste
1 tbsp (15 mL) cornstarch
1 tbsp (15 mL) water
1 tsp (5 mL) sesame oil
Salt and ground black pepper
2 green onions, finely chopped

Trim all visible fat from pork and cut into thin slices across grain. Stack slices and cut into thin strips.

Place pork in a large saucepan. Add mushrooms, carrot, water chestnuts, ginger, broth, vinegar, soy sauce and pepper sauce. Bring to a boil. Reduce heat, cover and simmer for 5 minutes.

In a small bowl, mix together cornstarch and water. Stir into soup and cook, stirring constantly, for 1 to 2 minutes or until thickened and bubbly. Stir in sesame oil. Add salt and pepper to taste. Garnish each serving with green onions.

Makes 2 servings, about 1 $1/4$ cups (300 mL) each.

Sesame Oil

Extracted from sesame seeds, sesame oil has a delicious nutty flavour. Roasting the seeds before pressing gives a darker oil with a stronger flavour. Just a small amount of the darker oil is all that is needed to bring a hint of Asia.

PER SERVING	
Amount	% Daily Value
Calories 267	
Fat 9g	14%
Saturated 2.4g	12%
Monounsaturated 2.7g	
Polyunsaturated 1.5g	
Sodium 308mg	13%
Carbohydrate 27g	9%
Fibre 2g	8%
Protein 23g	
Calcium 58mg	5%

Sherried Cream of Broccoli and Other Vegetable Soups

Preparation Time: 5 minutes Cook Time: 15 minutes

There are two essentials to a good broccoli soup. First, the broth needs to be rich and full-bodied, and second, the vegetables must not be overcooked. Homemade broth is the best way to achieve the first (see page 129) and cooking the vegetables separately in a microwave accomplishes the second. This recipe provides a guide to delicious soups using different garden vegetables.

2 tbsp (25 mL) butter or margarine
1 large onion, chopped
1/4 cup (50 mL) all-purpose flour
3 cups (750 mL) low-sodium chicken broth
4 cups (1 L) fresh or frozen broccoli pieces
1 cup (250 mL) milk
2 tbsp (25 mL) sherry (optional)
Salt and ground black pepper

In a large saucepan, heat butter over medium heat. Add onion. Cook for 10 minutes or until very soft. Stir in flour, mixing well. Add broth and bring to a boil, stirring constantly. Cook for 1 minute or until thickened and bubbly.

Meanwhile, rinse broccoli in water, drain and place in a large microwave-safe container. Microwave on 100% power for 5 minutes or just until tender. Add to saucepan along with any liquid.

Using a stick blender, process soup until smooth. Stir in milk and sherry. Add salt and pepper to taste and heat until hot but not boiling. Or place soup in a blender container and process until smooth. Return to saucepan and stir in milk and sherry. Heat to serving temperature and add salt and pepper to taste.

Makes 4 servings, about 1 1/4 cups (300 mL) each.

Variation: Cream of Cauliflower Soup

Replace broccoli with 3 cups (750 mL) cauliflower florets.

Variation: Cream of Asparagus Soup

Replace broccoli with 3 cups (750 mL) asparagus pieces. Cook as for broccoli, but reduce microwave cooking time from 5 to 3 minutes.

Variation: Cream of Mushroom Soup

Replace broccoli with 8 oz (250 g) sliced fresh mushrooms. Increase butter to 3 tbsp (45 mL) and cook mushrooms with onion.

Variation: Cream of Carrot Soup

Replace broccoli with 3 cups (750 mL) sliced carrots. Add carrots with broth and increase cooking time to 15 minutes.

Processing Pointers

Most food processors do not have liquid-tight lids, so a blender works best for puréeing soups. To use a food processor, strain the solids from the liquid and process the solids until smooth, then add back to the liquid. Another method is to put both liquid and solids through a food mill. A hand-held stick blender is the most convenient option for puréeing a soup.

Soup With Lentils, Fresh Herbs and Kale

Preparation Time: 10 minutes Cook Time: 1 ¼ hours

It is hard to find soup that is more in keeping with a healthy diet than this one. Made with a whole grain along with lentils and a red, yellow and green vegetable, it offers protein as well as generous portions of nutrients. The slow heating of the vegetables brings out their rich, tantalizing flavour, making an exceptional backdrop for the kale. For added interest, replace some of the brown rice with wild rice or quinoa.

1 tbsp (15 mL) olive oil

1 clove garlic, minced

1 onion, diced

1 small sweet potato, peeled and diced

½ cup (125 mL) dried brown lentils, rinsed

⅓ cup (75 mL) brown rice

2 large tomatoes, peeled and diced, about 2 cups (500 mL)

4 cups (1 L) low-sodium chicken or vegetable broth

1 ½ tsp (7 mL) chopped fresh oregano or ½ tsp (2 mL) dried

1 ½ tsp (7 mL) chopped fresh basil or ½ tsp (2 mL) dried

2 cups (500 mL) chopped kale, fibrous stems removed

Salt and ground black pepper

In a large saucepan, heat oil over medium heat. Add garlic, onion and sweet potato. Cook for 8 minutes or until soft, stirring frequently.

Add lentils, rice, tomatoes, broth, oregano and basil. Bring to a boil. Reduce heat, cover and simmer for 1 hour or until lentils are tender.

Stir in kale. Return to a boil and simmer for 5 minutes or until kale is tender. Add salt and pepper to taste.

Makes 4 servings, about 1 ¾ cups (425 mL) each.

Kale

Featuring attractive leaves, kale is often used as an ornamental garden plant. But it is also a nutritional superstar. A member of the cabbage family, it brings along the same bundle of nutrients associated with its better-known relatives. Younger leaves are tender and make a spicy addition to a salad. Larger, older leaves are perfect for adding to soup as they will stand up to longer cooking.

Amount	% Daily Value
Calories 285	
Fat 6g	9%
Saturated 1.1g	6%
Monounsaturated 2.8g	
Polyunsaturated 0.8g	
Sodium 114mg	5%
Carbohydrate 46g	15%
Fibre 6g	24%
Protein 15g	
Calcium 81mg	7%

Turkey Soup with Fresh Sage, Sweet Potato and Kale

Preparation Time: 15 minutes Cook Time: 25 minutes

Turkey stars as a delightful soup the day after the big dinner. Be sure to save the bones for making the broth base for this soup (see page 129).

1 tbsp (15 mL) canola oil
1 leek, white part only, thinly sliced
1 tbsp (15 mL) chopped fresh sage, or
    1 tsp (5 mL) dried
4 cups (1 L) low-sodium chicken
    broth or homemade turkey stock
1 large sweet potato, peeled and
    diced, about 12 oz (375 g)
1 cup (250 mL) cut-up cooked turkey
1 cup (250 mL) fresh or frozen cut
    green beans
1 cup (250 mL) chopped kale, fibrous
    stems removed
Salt and ground black pepper

In a large saucepan, heat oil over medium heat. Add leek and sage. Cook for 5 minutes or until leek is soft.

Add broth and sweet potato. Bring to a boil. Reduce heat, cover and simmer for 10 minutes or until sweet potato is tender.

Add turkey, green beans and kale. Bring to a boil, reduce heat, cover and simmer for 6 minutes or until the beans and kale are tender. Add salt and pepper to taste.

Makes 4 servings, 1 1/2 cup (375 mL) each.

Sweet Potatoes

In spite of the name, sweet potatoes contain about the same number of calories as white potatoes. But they star as a source of beta carotene. Sweet potatoes bruise easily and tend to spoil rapidly. Store them in a cook dry place for up to a week, never in the refrigerator where they may develop an off taste. To enjoy sweet potatoes as a simple side dish, mash cooked sweet potatoes with a bit of orange or pineapple juice seasoned with a sprinkle of nutmeg, cinnamon and ginger. With their sweet taste, they don't need the extra calories of traditional potato toppings.

PER SERVING	
Amount	% Daily Value
Calories 236	
Fat 8g	12%
Saturated 1.8g	9%
Monounsaturated 2.7g	
Polyunsaturated 2.0g	
Sodium 146mg	6%
Carbohydrate 18g	6%
Fibre 3g	12%
Protein 24g	
Calcium 91mg	8%

Maritime Clam Chowder

Preparation Time: 5 minutes Cook Time: 25 minutes

A quick version of a favourite chowder popular in New England and Canadian Maritime provinces. Canned clams provide great convenience, but use fresh clams if you can find them.

2 slices bacon, diced
2 stalks celery, chopped
1 onion, chopped
1 large potato, peeled and diced
1 1/2 cups (375 mL) low-sodium chicken broth
1 tbsp (15 mL) chopped fresh thyme, or 1 tsp (5 mL) dried
1 1/2 cups (375 mL) 2% milk
3 tbsp (45 mL) all-purpose flour
1 can (5 oz/140 mL) baby clams, drained
2 green onions, chopped

In a large saucepan, cook bacon over medium heat until brown and crisp, about 5 minutes.

Drain off and discard all but 1 tsp (5 mL) bacon fat. Add celery and onion to pan. Cook for 2 minutes or until slightly soft. Add potato, broth and thyme. Bring to a boil. Reduce heat, cover and cook for 15 minutes or until vegetables are tender.

In a small bowl, whisk together milk and flour. Whisk into soup and cook, stirring constantly, until it comes to a boil, about 2 minutes. Stir in clams and heat to serving temperature. Ladle into serving bowls and garnish with green onions.

Makes 4 servings, about 1 1/2 cups (375 mL) each.

PER SERVING	
Amount	**% Daily Value**
Calories 216	
Fat 4g	6%
Saturated 1.8g	9%
Monounsaturated 1.3g	
Polyunsaturated 0.5g	
Sodium 190mg	8%
Carbohydrate 29g	10%
Fibre 2g	8%
Protein 16g	
Calcium 166mg	15%

A Clam Chowder Chronicle

A chowder is generally thought of as a thick, rich soup with the ingredients in large pieces. But geographical regions have very definite traditions when it comes to versions with clams. Clam chowder made with a milk or cream base with potatoes, onion, bacon (or salt pork) and, of course, clams, probably originated along the east coast of Canada and New England where it has been popular since the mid-eighteenth century. In the early 1900s it also became popular further south, but there it took on a new identity. Portuguese immigrants in Rhode Island, no doubt remembering the thick tomato-based fish soups of their homeland, began adding tomatoes to this popular soup. This was heresy to traditional Maritimers. In 1939, a bill was introduced into the Maine legislature making the addition of tomatoes to clam chowder illegal. The tomato-based version eventually became known as "Manhattan-style" clam chowder and today restaurants typically serve one version, but never both.

Mixed Mushroom Soup with Fresh Thyme and Leeks ◼◤

Preparation Time: 5 minutes Cook Time: 50 minutes

An ambrosial soup to indulge mushroom lovers! Choose dark brown mushrooms such as crimini, portabella and shiitake for a full meaty flavour. A bit of barley gives an underlying richness.

2 tsp (10 mL) canola oil

1/2 cup (125 mL) thinly sliced leek (white and pale green parts only)

1/4 cup (50 mL) thinly sliced celery

2 cups (500 mL) sliced mixed mushrooms, (crimini, stemmed shiitake, oyster), about 5 oz (150 g)

2 cups (500 mL) low-sodium beef or vegetable broth

2 tbsp (25 mL) white wine

2 tbsp (25 mL) pearl barley

1 tsp (5 mL) chopped fresh thyme or 1/4 tsp (1 mL) dried

Salt and ground black pepper

In a large saucepan, heat oil over medium heat. Add leek and celery and cook for 3 minutes, stirring frequently. Add mushrooms. Cook for 5 minutes or until vegetables are slightly soft.

Add broth, wine, barley and thyme. Bring to a boil, reduce heat, cover and boil gently for about 40 minutes or until barley is tender. Add salt and pepper to taste.

Makes 2 servings, 1 1/2 cups (375 mL) each.

Barley: Hulled or Pearl?

Barley kernels are tough grains. Each kernel comes wrapped in three layers: two inedible husks that shield the germ (or embryo) of the plant and another layer known as the aleurone, which protects the endosperm, the starchy part of the grain. Animals can eat the unrefined grain, but humans cannot digest the husk. Thus, for human consumption, barley is polished, a process whereby the husks and often much of the aleurone and embryo are removed. This process takes place in stages. When part of the aleurone is left on the grain, it is known as hulled or pot barley. Removing all the aleurone and embryo produces pearl barley. Pearl barley has lost some of the nutrients, but it will cook in much less time than hulled. Both offer significant amounts of carbohydrate, fibre and protein as well as niacin, potassium, and thiamine. To use hulled barley in this recipe, place the barley in a 2-cup (500 mL) glass measure and fill with cold water. Microwave on 100% power until boiling and let stand for 1 hour before adding to soup. Increase cooking time to 1 hour.

PER SERVING	
Amount	**% Daily Value**
Calories 152	
Fat 6g	9%
Saturated 0.8g	4%
Monounsaturated 2.7g	
Polyunsaturated 1.5g	
Sodium 85mg	4%
Carbohydrate 17g	6%
Fibre 2g	8%
Protein 7g	
Calcium 32mg	3%

Fish Chowder with Vegetables

Preparation Time: 5 minutes Cook Time: 30 minutes

This warming soup is thought to have originated in Newfoundland in the 1700s where Breton fishermen would throw some of the day's catch into a large pot along with anything else on hand. In time, the French words *chaudron* for "pot" and *chaud* for "hot" became known as "chowder," a fish soup popular up and down the eastern coast of North America. Some fresh-baked bread is all that is needed for a satisfying meal. Use any combination of frozen or canned fish you have on hand.

1 tbsp (15 mL) butter or margarine
1 small onion, chopped
$1/2$ cup (125 mL) chopped celery
$1/2$ cup (125 mL) chopped carrot
1 cup (250 mL) water
1 $1/2$ cup (375 mL) diced raw potato
1 tsp (5 mL) chopped fresh thyme, or
   $1/4$ tsp (1 mL) dried
8 oz (250 g) fish fillets, cut in pieces
   (sole, cod, haddock or whitefish)
1 cup (250 mL) frozen peas
1 can (14 oz/385 mL) 2% evaporated
   milk
$1/2$ tsp (2 mL) Worcestershire sauce
Salt and ground black pepper

In a large saucepan, melt butter over medium heat. Add onion, celery and carrots. Cook for 5 minutes or until soft. Add water, potato and thyme. Bring to a boil. Reduce heat, cover and simmer for 15 minutes or until potato is almost tender.

Add fish. Return to boil and simmer for 5 minutes or until fish flakes easily.

Add peas. Return to boil. Stir in milk and Worcestershire sauce. Heat thoroughly, but do not allow to boil. Add salt and pepper to taste.

Makes 4 servings, about 1 $1/4$ cup (300 mL) each.

Bone Up

Bone up on calcium with this east coast delight, a tasty way to help reach your daily requirement for this important nutrient. For other ways to connect with calcium, see page 10 in the Introduction.

PER SERVING	
Amount	% Daily Value
Calories 253	
Fat 6	9%
Saturated 3.2g	16%
Monounsaturated 1.6g	
Polyunsaturated 0.5g	
Sodium 251mg	10%
Carbohydrate 29g	10%
Fibre 3g	12%
Protein 21g	
Calcium 308mg	28%

Portuguese Kielbasa and Cabbage Soup

Preparation Time: 15 minutes Cook Time: 35 minutes

A delicious hearty soup from the Ribatejo province of Portugal. It is known locally as Sopa de Pedra or stone soup from a legend about a beggar who asked a poor couple for something to eat. When they pointed to their bare cupboard, he began to make a soup with stones. Suggesting the soup would be better with an onion, one was found and added to the pot followed by a carrot, and then other ingredients until there was enough for a tasty soup. Here the kidney beans represent the stones. Follow the beggar's philosophy and use whatever vegetables you have on hand to replace those here. We've planned 6 servings as this soup is even better reheated the next day.

1 tbsp (15 mL) olive oil
2 to 4 oz (60 to 125 g) Kielbassa
  or other spicy cooked sausage,
  chopped
2 onions, chopped
2 large carrots, diced
2 parsnips, diced
2 potatoes, diced
2 cups (500 mL) coarsely chopped
  cabbage
2 cups (500 mL) low-sodium beef or
  vegetable broth
2 cups (500 mL) water
1 bay leaf
2 cups (500 mL) cooked red kidney
  beans, or 1 can (19 oz/540 mL)
  kidney beans, drained and rinsed
$1/4$ cup (50 mL) chopped fresh parsley,
  or 1 $1/2$ tbsp (22 mL) dried
Salt and ground black pepper

In a large saucepan, heat oil over medium heat. Cook sausage and onion for 4 minutes or until onion is transparent. Add carrots and parsnips. Cook for 10 minutes or until vegetables are slightly soft.

Add potatoes, cabbage, broth, water and bay leaf. Bring to a boil. Reduce heat, cover and simmer for 20 minutes or until vegetables are tender.

Add kidney beans and parsley. Return to boiling. Discard bay leaf and add salt and pepper to taste.

Makes 6 servings, about 1 $1/2$ cups (375 mL) each.

PER SERVING	
Amount	% Daily Value
Calories 243	
Fat 5g	8%
Saturated 1.1g	6%
Monounsaturated 2.4g	
Polyunsaturated 0.7g	
Sodium 294mg	12%
Carbohydrate 42g	14%
Fibre 9g	36%
Protein 12g	
Calcium 107mg	10%

Worth Its Salt

Salt has enhanced the taste of foods since antiquity. While sodium and chloride, the two major components of salt, are essential for our survival, it is easy to consume too much. Most prepared foods are high in salt and many cooks have heavy hands with the salt shaker. Salt is not the same as sodium, which makes up about 40 per cent of the salt crystal. And salt is not the only source of sodium in processed foods. To limit your intake, look for low-sodium or sodium-reduced products. One cup of regular chicken broth carries about 760 mg of sodium compared to 553 mg in sodium-reduced broth and only 72 mg in low-sodium broth. Refer to the Introduction (page 5) for more about salt and sodium.

Fagioli

Preparation Time: 10 minutes Cook Time: 35 minutes

Fagioli is a classic soup from Italy featuring beans and pasta with vegetables in a flavourful broth. This version includes a bit of pesto (either commercial or make Presto Pesto on page 92) for added flavour. The combination of beans and pasta makes for a delicious meal as well as a complete protein. Serve with some crusty Italian bread.

1 tbsp (15 mL) olive oil
1/2 cup (125 mL) chopped onions
1/2 cup (125 mL) chopped carrot
1/2 cup (125 mL) chopped celery
1 tbsp (15 mL) finely chopped garlic
2 1/2 cups (625 mL) water
2 cups (500 mL) low-sodium beef broth
1 can (19 oz/540 mL) diced no-salt-added tomatoes
3 stalks kale, stems and leaves chopped separately
2 tbsp (25 mL) pesto
1/3 cup (75 mL) chopped fresh parsley, or 2 tbsp (25 mL) dried
1 tbsp (15 mL) chopped fresh basil, or 1 tsp (5 mL) dried
1 1/2 tsp (7 mL) chopped fresh thyme, or 1/2 tsp (2 mL) dried
1 tsp (5 mL) granulated sugar
1/8 tsp (1/2 mL) ground black pepper
2 cups (500 mL) cooked red kidney beans or 1 can (19 oz/540 mL) kidney beans, rinsed and drained
1/2 cup (125 mL) small shell pasta or macaroni
3 tbsp (45 mL) grated Parmesan cheese

In a large saucepan, heat oil over medium heat. Cook onions, carrots, celery and garlic for 5 minutes.

Stir in water, broth, tomatoes, kale stems, pesto, parsley, basil, thyme, sugar and pepper. Bring to a boil. Reduce heat, cover and simmer for 20 minutes or until vegetables are soft.

Stir in beans, pasta and kale leaves. Bring to a boil, reduce heat, cover and simmer for 10 minutes or until pasta is tender but firm. Spoon into bowls and sprinkle with cheese.

Makes 6 servings, 1 1/2 cup (375 mL) each.

Tomatoes in the Can

Look for tomatoes labelled "no salt added" to help keep sodium in check. And when fresh tomatoes are plentiful, use 2 cups (500 mL) chopped, peeled fresh tomatoes for the 19 oz/540 mL can.

PER SERVING	
Amount	% Daily Value
Calories 231	
Fat 8g	12%
Saturated 1.8g	9%
Monounsaturated 4.7g	
Polyunsaturated 0.9g	
Sodium 260mg	11%
Carbohydrate 30g	10%
Fibre 6g	24%
Protein 11g	
Calcium 177mg	16%

HAPPY ENDINGS

A happy ending to a meal brings joy to both the eye and the palate and adds a pleasant note in the total day's nutritional harmony. Fruit rates high on all of these accounts. So, not surprisingly, it is featured prominently in our sweet suggestions.

Plentiful all year long and convenient to buy in small quantity, fresh fruit fits perfectly into a meal plan for two. A bowl filled with the pick of the season is the simplest of happy endings. Dried fruit and frozen berries can be on hand to give variety. Be sure to try our Simple Fruit Desserts for Two for fruit with an added touch.

Other champion performers for happy endings are dairy products. By dessert time, if you have not had your full measure of calcium, it's smart to opt for yogurt, milk, custard and occasionally cheese or ice cream. These pair perfectly with fruit, giving double goodness.

For a celebration dinner, something special is in order. Fruit Crumble Singles (page 152) and Berry Pie for Two with No-Roll Pastry and Crumb Topping (page 154) are enticing solutions to the dessert challenge and meet the golden rule of great taste, great appeal and smart choice.

Dessert often spells sweetness and creaminess, two wonderful attributes bound to carry with them a bundle of calories. Wise choice of ingredients and attention to portion sizes will go a long way in containing the calorie count. Consequently, we have opted for yogurt in our mouth-watering Raspberry Yogurt Parfait (page 146) and Mango Fool with Blueberries (page 150). We invite you to follow our lead.

Raspberry Yogurt Parfait, Man
Fool with Blueberries, Fr
Crumble Singles, Winter Fr
Compote with Custard Sauc
Berry Pie for Two with No R
Pastry and Crumb Toppir
Simple Fruit Desserts for Tw
Raspberry Yogurt Parfait, Man
Fool with Blueberries, Fr
Crumble Singles, Winter Fr
Compote with Custard Sauc
Berry Pie for Two with No-R
Pastry and Crumb Toppir
Simple Fruit Desserts for Tw
Raspberry Yogurt Parfait, Man
Fool with Blueberries, Fr
Crumble Singles, Winter Fr
Compote with Custard Sauc
Berry Pie for Two with No-R
Pastry and Crumb Toppir
Simple Fruit Desserts for Tw
Raspberry Yogurt Parfait, Man
Fool with Blueberries, Fr
Crumble Singles, Winter Fr
Compote with Custard Sauc
Berry Pie for Two with No-R
Pastry and Crumb Toppir
Simple Fruit Desserts for Tw
Raspberry Yogurt Parfait, Man
Fool with Blueberries, Fr
Crumble Singles, Winter Fr
Compote with Custard Sauc
Berry Pie for Two with No-R
Pastry and Crumb Toppir
Simple Fruit Desserts for Tw
Raspberry Yogurt Parfait, Man
Fool with Blueberries, Fr
Crumble Singles, Winter Fr
Compote with Custard Sauc
Berry Pie for Two with No-R
Pastry and Crumb Toppin
Simple Fruit Desserts for Tw
Raspberry Yogurt Parfait, Man
Fool with Blueberries, Fr
Crumble Singles, Winter Fr
Compote with Custard Sau

SIMPLE FRUIT DESSERTS FOR TWO

Preparation Time: 5 minutes Cook Time: 0 to 20 minutes

For a no-fuss ending to a meal, simply bring a fruit bowl to the table at dessert time along with small knives for cutting. For a more elegant occasion, accompany the fruit with one or two kinds of cheese and plain crackers such as oat cakes or water crackers.

Select fruit that is free from bruises and with different degrees of ripeness to meet your needs. Wash thoroughly in water to remove dirt and any pesticide residues. There is no need to use any special product or to be especially concerned with the wax finish that may have been applied to protect the fruit.

To add interesting taste to fruit, try these suggestions. Each brings one serving from the vegetables and fruit food group. Each dessert makes two servings.

Ricotta Cream Topping for Fruit

1/4 cup (50 mL) ricotta cheese
2 tbsp (10 mL) icing sugar
Grated lemon zest, crystallized ginger,
    vanilla extract
2 peaches, nectarines or plums
    or 1 cup (250 mL) strawberries,
    raspberries or blueberries

In a small bowl, combine cheese with icing sugar. Add a bit of lemon zest, crystallized ginger and vanilla if desired. Spoon over fresh fruit such as a sliced peach or over blueberries, strawberries and raspberries.

Raspberries in Chambord with Ice Cream

1 cup (250 mL) fresh or defrosted
    frozen raspberries
1 tbsp (15 mL) superfine (fruit) sugar
1 tbsp (15 mL) Chambord liqueur or
    kirsch brandy
1 cup (250 mL) ice cream or frozen
    yogurt

In a small bowl, combine raspberries and sugar. Let stand for 20 minutes. Stir in liqueur. Spoon over ice cream or frozen yogurt.

Caribbean Bananas

1 peeled banana, sliced
1 peeled seedless orange, sliced
4 tsp (20 mL) brown sugar
2 tsp (10 mL) rum
Ice cream or frozen yogurt (optional)

Divide banana and orange between 2 small microwave-safe custard cups. Sprinkle each with half of the brown sugar and half of the rum. Microwave on 100% power for 1 1/2 to 2 minutes or until banana is slightly soft. Top with ice cream or frozen yogurt if desired.

Warm Peach Gratin

2 peaches or nectarines
$^1/_2$ cup (125 mL) vanilla yogurt
1 tsp (5 mL) lightly packed brown
   sugar

Preheat broiler. Slice 1 peach or nectarine into each of 2 small microwave-safe custard cups. Spread each with $^1/_4$ cup (50 mL) vanilla yogurt and sprinkle with $^1/_2$ tsp (2 mL) brown sugar. Broil for 2 minutes or until sugar is bubbly. Serve immediately.

Maple Bananas

2 bananas
2 tbsp (25 mL) maple syrup

Slice 1 banana into each of 2 small serving dishes. Pour maple syrup over each. If desired, microwave on 100% power for 40 seconds or just until banana is hot.

Amaretti Apples or Pears

2 apples or pears
1 tsp (5 mL) granulated sugar
10 amaretti cookies (available in most
   Italian supermarkets)
$^1/_4$ cup (50 mL) vanilla yogurt or ice
   cream

Peel and slice 1 apple or pear into each of 2 microwave-safe custard cups. Sprinkle each with half the sugar. Crush the cookies and sprinkle over fruit. Microwave on 100% power for 2 to 2 $^1/_2$ minutes or until fruit is soft. Serve with a dollop of vanilla yogurt or ice cream.

Strawberries in Red Wine

1 $^1/_2$ cups (375 mL) sliced strawberries
2 tbsp (25 mL) granulated sugar
2 tbsp (25 mL) dry red wine
$^1/_4$ cup (50 mL) frozen yogurt or ice
   cream

In a medium bowl, combine strawberries and sugar. Let berries stand for 4 to 10 hours. Drain liquid into a small microwave-safe container. Add wine. microwave on 100% power for 40 seconds or until boiling. Divide strawberries between two serving dishes and pour sauce over berries. Top with a dollop of frozen yogurt or ice cream.

Orange Ambrosia

2 large seedless oranges
$^1/_4$ cup (50 mL) shredded
   unsweetened coconut
1 tsp (5 mL) fruit sugar

In a small bowl, combine the grated zest from 1 orange with coconut and sugar. Peel both oranges and slice into circles. Layer oranges and coconut mixture in 2 small serving dishes ending with a layer of coconut. Chill several hours.

Pears in Port

1/2 cup (125 mL) port wine
1/4 cup (50 mL) granulated sugar
2 pears, peeled and halved

In a small saucepan, bring wine and sugar to a boil. Add pears. Reduce heat, cover and simmer for 20 minutes, or until pears are soft and translucent. Remove pears. Continue boiling syrup until about 2 tbsp (25 mL) remains. Pour over pears and chill until serving time.

Apple Bake

2 apples
2 tsp (10 mL) lightly packed brown sugar
Dash ground cinnamon
2 tsp (10 mL) red currant jelly
1/4 cup (50 mL) vanilla yogurt or ice cream

Peel, core and slice 1 apple into each of two small microwave-safe serving dishes. Mix each with half the brown sugar and a dash of cinnamon. Dot each with half the jelly. Microwave on 100% power for 2 to 2 1/2 minutes or until apples are soft. Serve with a dollop of vanilla yogurt or ice cream.

Fruit with Chocolate Fondue

4 tsp (20 mL) half-and-half (10%) cream
2 oz (60 g) semi-sweet chocolate, cut in pieces
Assorted cubes of fresh fruit (apples, pears, bananas, strawberries, orange segments, pineapple chunks)

In a glass measuring cup, place cream and chocolate. Microwave on 40% power for 2 minutes or until chocolate is melted. Serve with an assortment of fresh fruit for dipping.

Grilled Fruit Kabobs

2 peaches, plums or nectarines, cut in large pieces
2 tbsp (25 mL) maple syrup
1/2 cup (250 mL) ice cream or frozen yogurt

Preheat grill to hot. Thread pieces of peaches, plums or nectarines on soaked wooden skewers. Brush fruit with maple syrup and grill for about 1 minute per side or until lightly caramelized. Serve with ice cream or frozen yogurt.

Pineapple and Strawberries with Maple Syrup

1/2 small fresh pineapple, peeled and cored
2 tbsp (25 mL) pure maple syrup
1 1/2 tsp (7 mL) fresh lemon juice
1 tsp (5 mL) Chambord or kirsch liqueur (optional)
6 to 8 strawberries, sliced

Cut pineapple crosswise into slices. Arrange on serving plate. Combine syrup, lemon juice and liqueur (if using) and pour over pineapple. Scatter strawberries over pineapple.

Raspberry Yogurt Parfait 📹

Preparation Time: 5 minutes

Parfait means "perfect" in French and is usually a layered dessert with ice cream and a sweet syrup or fruit sauce. An equally perfect dessert uses yogurt and a purée of fresh raspberries. Another time use a mango or fresh peaches for a delicious variation.

½ cup (125 mL) fresh or frozen
  raspberries
2 tsp (10 mL) superfine (fruit) sugar
1 tsp (5 mL) fresh lemon juice
½ cup (125 mL) plain or vanilla
  yogurt
Whole raspberries for garnish

In a food processor, process raspberries, sugar and lemon juice until very smooth.

Into each of two parfait glasses, alternate layers of raspberry purée and yogurt. Or, into each of two small serving dishes, spoon half of the raspberry purée and half of the yogurt. Draw the tip of a knife gently through the surface to create a swirl pattern. Garnish each dessert with a few whole raspberries. Chill until serving time.

Makes 2 servings.

Yogurt

Yogurt is a cultured milk product that dates back to before the common era. Nomadic peoples in the Balkan peninsula are thought to have discovered the process of coagulating milk, probably first by accident and then as a means of preservation. Yogurt has been a dietary staple in European countries for years, more recently gaining popularity in North America. To make yogurt, milk from cows as well as sheep and goats is cultured with various strains of lactobacillus, a friendly bacteria, which produces a mild acid that coagulates the protein. Some brands have stabilizers such as gelatin added to keep the yogurt from separating. Plain yogurt without stabilizers can be made slightly thicker by placing it in a sieve to allow some of the liquid to drain away. Greek-style yogurt already has part of the liquid or whey removed, resulting in a thick creamy product. But since some of the calcium is lost in the whey, Greek-style yogurt has about 20 per cent less calcium than regular yogurt.

PER SERVING	
Amount	**% Daily Value**
Calories 76	
Fat 1g	2%
Saturated 0.6g	3%
Monounsaturated 0.3g	
Polyunsaturated 0.1g	
Sodium 43mg	2%
Carbohydrate 14g	5%
Fibre 3g	12%
Protein 4g	
Calcium 122mg	11%

Winter Fruit Compote with Custard Sauce 🎥

Preparation Time: 5 minutes Standing Time: 60 minutes Cook Time: 10 minutes

A mixture of dried fruit cooked slowly with a hint of orange makes a happy ending to a winter meal. Use any combination of dried fruit and serve warm or chilled. Topped with vanilla yogurt, the compote is also delicious for a special-occasion breakfast.

¼ cup (50 mL) dried apricots

¼ cup (50 mL) pitted prunes

¼ cup (50 mL) dried sliced apples

2 tbsp (25 mL) dried cranberries, blueberries or cherries

⅓ cup (75 mL) orange juice

2 tbsp (25 mL) brown sugar

1 tbsp (15 mL) fresh lemon juice

2 tsp (10 mL) chopped crystallized ginger

In a small saucepan, combine apricots, prunes, apples and cranberries. Add orange juice, brown sugar, lemon juice and ginger. Cover and let stand for 1 hour.

Bring to a boil. Reduce heat, cover and simmer for 10 minutes or until fruit is tender. Cool and serve slightly warm, or refrigerate and serve cold. Serve with custard sauce.

Makes 2 servings.

Microwave Custard Sauce

The secret to making a very quick custard sauce in your microwave is to use low power, stir frequently and not allow the custard to boil.

¼ cup (50 mL) milk

1 egg yolk

1 tbsp (15 mL) granulated sugar

½ tsp (2 mL) cornstarch

¼ tsp (1 mL) vanilla

In a 1-cup (250 mL) glass measuring cup or microwave-safe container, whisk together milk, egg yolk, sugar and cornstarch until well blended.

Microwave custard on 30% power for 45 seconds. Stir with a small metal spoon and continue to microwave on 30% power, stirring every 10 seconds, until just thickened and the custard coats the spoon, about 30 seconds longer. Watch carefully to be sure mixture does not boil. Stir in vanilla.

Makes about ⅓ cup (75 mL).

Keep It Fresh

To keep fresh lemon juice on hand, place 1-tablespoon (15 mL) amounts of juice into individual ice cube containers and freezer. Remove the frozen cubes and store them in a plastic bag. The flavour of fresh juice is far superior to the bottled kind.

PER SERVING	
Amount	**% Daily Value**
Calories 303	
Fat 4g	6%
Saturated 1.2g	6%
Monounsaturated 1.3g	
Polyunsaturated 0.4g	
Sodium 37mg	2%
Carbohydrate 68g	23%
Fibre 4g	16%
Protein 4g	
Calcium 97mg	9%

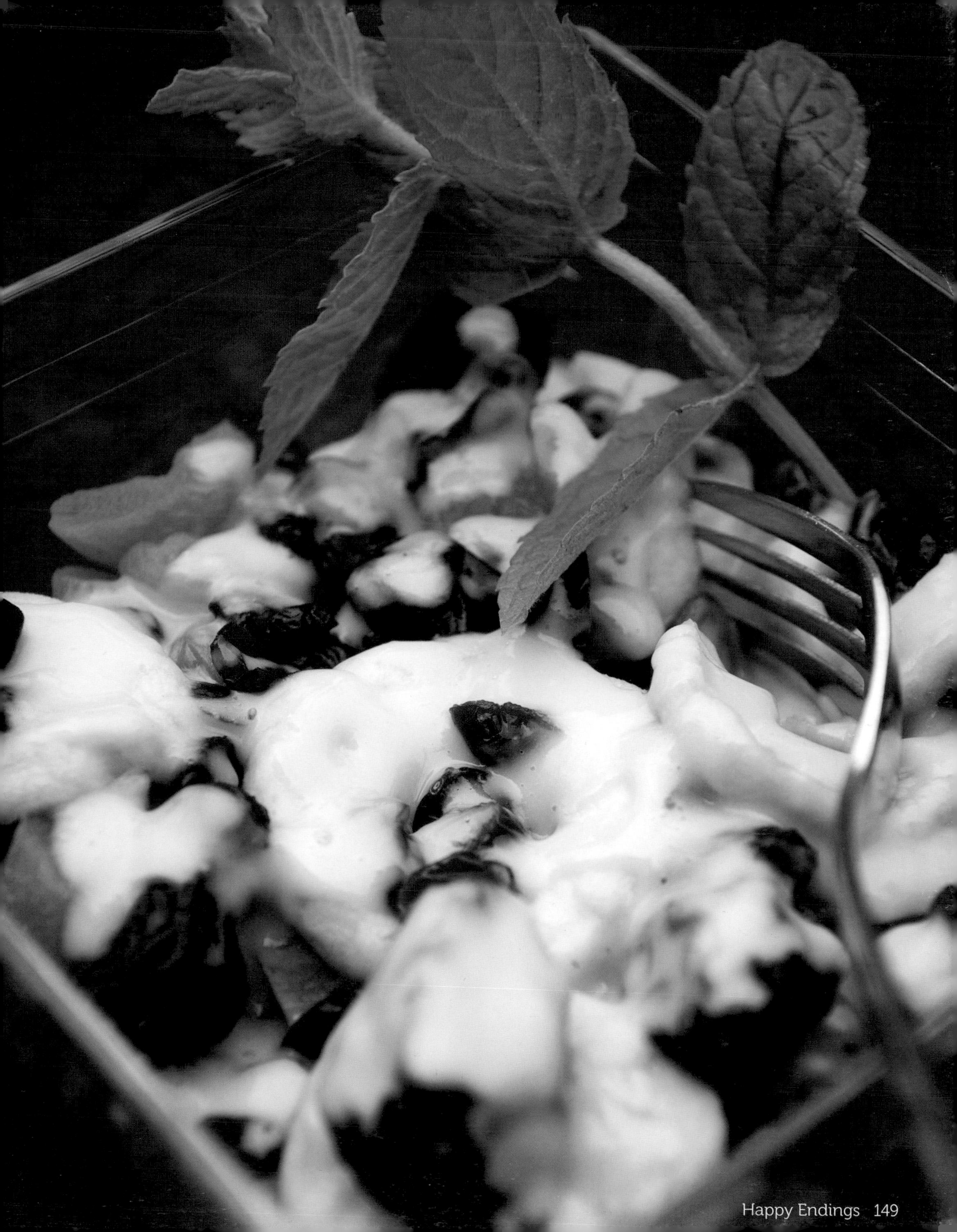

Mango Fool with Blueberries

Standing Time: 2 hours Preparation Time: 10 minutes

Fresh mango and colourful blueberries combine for this delicious and refreshing ending to a meal. For a striking presentation, serve with a simple crisp cookie on the side.

³/₄ cups (175 mL) plain yogurt
1 tbsp (15 mL) superfine (fruit) sugar
1 mango, peeled and cut into chunks
Grated zest and juice from 1 lime
2 tbsp (25 mL) blueberries

Place yogurt in a large sieve lined with cheesecloth. Set over a bowl and allow to drip for 2 hours in the refrigerator. Discard liquid and transfer yogurt into bowl. Stir in sugar.

In a food processor or blender, place mango (reserving a few pieces for garnish), lime zest and lime juice. Process until smooth. Fold into yogurt.

Spoon mixture into glass serving dishes. Dice reserved mango. Top each dish with a bit of mango and a few blueberries.

Makes 2 servings.

Fine Fools

Seventeenth-century England was the place of origin of this old-fashioned dessert made from puréed fruit folded into whipped cream. Gooseberries were the traditional choice, but any fruit may be substituted. Firm yogurt makes an equally delicious version with far fewer calories and a bonus of calcium.

Amount	% Daily Value
Calories 156	
Fat 2g	3%
Saturated 1.0g	5%
Monounsaturated 0.5g	
Polyunsaturated 0.1g	
Sodium 66mg	3%
Carbohydrate 32g	11%
Fibre 2g	8%
Protein 5g	
Calcium 146mg	13%

Fruit Crumble Singles

Preparation Time: 10 minutes Cook Time: 1 minute

With a crumbly oatmeal topping made ahead, your choice of fruit is the basis of a quick celestial dessert. Serve with a dollop of vanilla yogurt or ice cream.

¾ cup (175 mL) diced fruit (see combinations below)

1 tsp (5 mL) brown or granulated sugar

¼ cup (50 mL) Topping Mix (recipe below)

In a small microwave-safe cup, place fruit and mix with sugar. Sprinkle topping mix over and microwave on 100% power for 1 minute or until fruit is soft. For two fruit crumbles, microwave for 2 minutes.

Makes 1 serving.

Fruit Combinations

Apple Crumble Single:
1 small apple, peeled, cored and sliced. 1 tsp (5 mL) dried currants

Pear Crumble Single:
1 small pear, peeled, cored and sliced. 1 tsp (5 mL) chopped crystalline ginger

Peach Crumble Single:
1 peach, peeled, pitted and sliced. 2 tbsp (25 mL) blueberries

Plum Blueberry Crumble Single:
1 red or purple plum, pitted and sliced. ¼ cup (50 mL) blueberries

Rhubarb Crumble Single:
¾ cup (175 mL) diced rhubarb

Rhubarb Strawberry Crumble Single:
½ cup (125 mL) diced rhubarb. ¼ cup (50 mL) sliced strawberries

Mango Crumble Single:
⅔ cup (150 mL) diced mango. 1 tbsp (15 mL) dried cranberries

Topping Mix

¾ cup (175 mL) quick-cooking rolled oats

¼ cup (50 mL) lightly packed brown sugar

2 tbsp (25 mL) toasted wheat germ (see page 7 for toasting instructions)

1 tbsp (15 mL) whole wheat flour

½ tsp (2 mL) ground cinnamon

1 tbsp (15 mL) melted butter or margarine

In a small bowl, combine oats, sugar, wheat germ, flour and cinnamon. Stir in butter and mix well. Store in refrigerator in a jar with a tight-fitting lid. Makes enough mix for 5 Fruit Crumble Singles.

PER SERVING OF APPLE
CRUMBLE SINGLE

Amount	% Daily Value
Calories 212	
Fat 4g	6%
Saturated 1.7g	9%
Monounsaturated 1.0g	
Polyunsaturated 0.7g	
Sodium 31mg	1%
Carbohydrate 45g	15%
Fibre 4g	16%
Protein 3g	
Calcium 33mg	3%

Berry Pie for Two with No-Roll Pastry and Crumb Topping

Preparation Time: 20 minutes Cook Time: 25 minutes

As no rolling is required, this very tender and crisp pastry is a snap to make for a small pie. And best of all, it uses heart-friendly canola oil.

Pastry:
½ cup (125 mL) all-purpose flour
¼ tsp (1 mL) granulated sugar
⅛ tsp (0.5 mL) baking powder
⅛ tsp (0.5 mL) salt
1 ½ tbsp (22 mL) canola oil
1 ½ tbsp (22 mL) milk

Filling:
¼ cup (50 mL) granulated sugar
1 ½ tbsp (22 mL) all-purpose flour
¾ cup (175 mL) fresh or frozen
   blueberries
¾ cup (175 mL) finely chopped
   rhubarb
1 tbsp (15 mL) lightly packed light
   brown sugar

Pastry:
In a 12-oz (375 mL) shallow glass dish, combine flour, sugar, baking powder and salt.

In a small bowl, whisk together oil and milk until well blended. Pour into flour mixture. Toss with a fork to mix. Add more milk or flour if needed to form crumbs that will stick together when pressed. Cover crumbs and let rest for 5 minutes or longer.

Remove 2 tablespoons (25 mL) of the crumb mixture and place in a small bowl. Using a fork and your fingers, pat remaining crumbs in a thin layer on bottom and sides of dish, forming a shell. Set aside.

Filling:
Preheat oven to 400°F (200°C). In a medium bowl, combine sugar and flour. Add blueberries and rhubarb, tossing gently to mix. Pour into pastry shell.

Mix brown sugar with reserved crumbs and sprinkle over top of filling. Bake for 25 minutes or until topping is browned and juice begins to bubble through.

Makes 2 servings.

Pastry Perfection

The role of making a tender pastry falls to the fat and different fats produce different results. Solid fat is left in coarse pieces that create thin layers in the flour-water dough, giving a flaky texture. Pastry made from oil is more crumbly. Blending milk with the oil in this pastry helps disperse the oil evenly, resulting in a very tender crust.

PER SERVING	
Amount	% Daily Value
Calories 396	
Fat 11g	17%
Saturated 1.0g	5%
Monounsaturated 6.2g	
Polyunsaturated 3.2g	
Sodium 184mg	8%
Carbohydrate 71g	24%
Fibre 3g	12%
Protein 5g	
Calcium 68mg	6%

Nutrient Analysis of Recipes and Main Meals

The recipes and meals were analysed using Food Smart Nutrition Management Solutions, Professional Edition software (Copyright ©Envision Health Networks, 2006). This software is based on the Canadian Nutrient File, 2005 and the USDA Nutrient Database for Standard Reference SR18, 2005.

Unless otherwise stated, recipes were analysed using 2% milk, 1 to 2% yogurt, large eggs and enriched pasta. It was assumed that only the lean portion of meat and poultry, without skin, would be eaten. Where several options were suggested in a recipe, the analysis was based on the first ingredient listed. Salt was included in the analysis only when a specific amount was listed. It was not included if salt was added "to taste." Optional ingredients and garnishes were not included in the nutrient analysis.

The "per serving" analysis lists the nutrients that are of general population interest and that have an impact on health such as fat, sodium and calcium. The gram values for carbohydrate and protein are included to provide an overview of the major nutrients from food. As there are many products on the market that could vary the nutrient values for recipes, the nutrient charts provide only a guideline. Sodium is a particular challenge in this respect.

We attempted to keep nutrients for the recipes within general guidelines for health by watching both the grams of fat, carbohydrate and protein along with the percent of calories they provided. Total fat was targeted between 20 and 35 per cent of calories. For most dinner meals, saturated fat was limited to 10 per cent of calories or less with carbohydrate providing between 40 and 60 per cent of the total energy.

For sodium, we used 2,400 mg per day as our reference to be consistent with food product labels, although the Adequate Intake (AI) is actually only 1,500 mg or less depending on age and other health factors. As well as monitoring the sodium in each recipe and meal, we looked at the sodium relative to the calories. Our objective was to keep the milligrams of sodium less than the number of calories and most of our recipes fall below this guideline. However, those with an Asian flavour using soy or fish sauces required a slightly higher limit. All single recipes in the book have less than 600 mg sodium per serving and the meals with side dishes followed the Heart and Stroke Foundation's Health Check Standard of under 720 mg of sodium for a dinner entree or mixed dish. Since appetizers, desserts and beverages were not included in the meal analysis, the total amount of sodium consumed will depend on the amount and choice of foods eaten during the full day.

INDEX

Acknowledgements

Fresh & Healthy Cooking for Two grew out of our need to serve tasty, healthy meals on a daily basis now that we are cooking for only two. From an initial working agreement, our relationship has evolved into a strong friendship as we collaborated over several years while developing recipes for meals with balanced nutrients and, most particularly, lower sodium levels.

A special thanks goes to our supportive and much-loved families who stood by us in this process and gave freely of their opinions and of their taste buds. Their input and critique were invaluable.

We also wish to acknowledge the following people who made significant contributions: Our many friends and colleagues who so kindly shared their favourite recipe ideas and especially our recipe testers Marjory Harvey, Barbara Herd and Karen Topp who prepared our recipes and offered their suggestions and comments. Marian Hebb who made contact with Formac Publishing and worked out the required legalities.

The Formac Publishing team who transformed our manuscript into a handsome finished book and especially to our editor, Christen Thomas, for her significant guidance and support.